you might find some
nuggets in here.
I hope so.
Chris

Life is a Bicycle

Life is a
Bicycle

If You Stop Pedaling You'll Fall Off

A Living Philosophy to
Finding your Authenticity

Garry Fitchett

NEW YORK

Life is a Bicycle

If You Stop Pedaling You'll Fall Off - A Living Philosophy to Finding your Authenticity

© 2016 Garry Fitchett

This publication is designed to provide competent, accurate and thought-provoking information with regard to the content herein. It is sold with the understanding that the author and publisher are not engaged in providing psychological, legal, financial, or other professional advice.

Published in New York, New York, by Morgan James Publishing. Morgan James and The Entrepreneurial Publisher are trademarks of Morgan James, LLC. www.MorganJamesPublishing.com

The Morgan James Speakers Group can bring authors to your live event. For more information or to book an event visit The Morgan James Speakers Group at www.TheMorganJamesSpeakersGroup.com.

ISBN 9781630477653 paperback
ISBN 9781630477660 eBook
ISBN 9781630477677 hardcover
Library of Congress Control Number:
2015914087

Shelfie

A **free** eBook edition is available with the purchase of this print book.

CLEARLY PRINT YOUR NAME ABOVE IN UPPER CASE

Instructions to claim your free eBook edition:
1. Download the Shelfie app for Android or iOS
2. Write your name in **UPPER CASE** above
3. Use the Shelfie app to submit a photo
4. Download your eBook to any device

Cover Design by:
Chris Treccani
www.3dogdesign.net

Interior Design by:
Chris Treccani
www.3dogdesign.net

In an effort to support local communities and raise awareness and funds, Morgan James Publishing donates a percentage of all book sales for the life of each book to Habitat for Humanity Peninsula and Greater Williamsburg.

Get involved today, visit
www.MorganJamesBuilds.com

To my wife, Julie, and my sons, Dylan and John: Watching you pursue your loves, interests, and passions with faith, fixity of purpose, and unbridled energy inspires me every day.

For all those souls who can't escape the feeling they were put on this Earth to do unique and meaningful work.

Contents

Preface

After graduating from the University of North Carolina at Chapel Hill with a master's degree in education, I abruptly chose not to teach. Instead I followed my heart and began a career in business. I was fortunate to work for burgeoning enterprises in an executive role and followed that by running a restaurant development company.

Loving business but recognizing my affinity for ideas that articulated the art and science of discovering one's professional best, I became intrigued. I grew compelled to learn more about what great minds of the past and present had to say on the subject of discovering their professional *true north*. Soon the torch was lit for my own authentic work. I wished to share what I learned and aspired to affect hearts and souls over temporal appetites. Therefore, I wrote a book that I could not find, but like you—needed to read.

In this book I venture to instill the inspirational idea that work's role is less to provide for the bare essentials of everyday life and more to fulfill the higher purpose of advancing our minds and unfolding our souls. *Life is a Bicycle* employs the bicycle and the act of cycling as a metaphor for finding and exercising genuine work because:

- Everyone is hard-wired to ride a bicycle.

- The bicycle's physical structure, principles of operation, techniques of deployment, and physics of motion comprise a veritable classroom on wheels. This is analogous to having a true and fulfilling career that displays one's essence.

    ☐   Once you learn to ride a bicycle, you never forget.

In the particular is contained the universal.

James Joyce
Irish novelist and poet

Discovering your proper career and profession (finding your bicycle) comes from understanding what it is you value most. Cheerful, spirited, and fulfilled people exercising their passion and creativity while striving for their personal best is something I value. My purpose is to inspire people to find and follow their authentic work. My work furnishes the reader with inspiration, practical principles and timeless philosophies so they may become an unobstructed channel between what they *will* and *love,* and what they *do.*

Your bicycle—your best work—can be found or created through your imagination, judgment, and intellect. Here you'll find the tools, signs, and guideposts necessary to discover and successfully navigate your cycling passageway. By diligently searching through the years for my own peerless and meritorious work, I developed a philosophy gleaned from the ideas and principles outlined in *Life is a Bicycle.*

There is nothing that will not reveal its secrets if you love it enough.

George Washington Carver
American scientist

My goal is to assist you, the curious reader, to claim your rightful seat on your singular bike; always and forever moving you from frustration to optimism—professionally, and by extension, throughout your life. A graceful rider on his unique bike, moving in the honest direction of a true purpose, is a thing of beauty.

Most people live lives of quiet desperation and go to their graves with the song still in them.

Henry David Thoreau
American author

Finding and following your work avoids this fate.

For those who seek:

Who is riding my bicycle?

Find your true and purposeful work—your *raison d'etre*—capable of advancing your mind, nourishing your body, and unfolding your soul. Then, claim it for yourself as the rightful owner.

Introduction

Historically, men and women have worked to provide the bare essentials for everyday life. *Life is a Bicycle* explores work's next generation of thought and examines its higher purpose: to nurture the advancing mind and unfold the soul. It is your birthright to express yourself harmoniously through your daily work.

Timeless philosophical thought is melded with the symbol of the bicycle in an effort to communicate a truth in the only way it can be successfully communicated—indirectly. The use of the bicycle endeavors to clothe the ideal of finding one's professional true north in a recognizable and perceptible form. It makes the metaphysical act of discovering one's authentic work physical, understandable, and therefore, actionable.

The ubiquitous and universally recognized bicycle becomes a metaphor for work: cycling, the act of performing one's work. Why? *Because life is a bicycle—if you stop pedaling, you'll fall off.* The bicycle captures the beauty and the essence of work through analogies, principles, and parallels.

Your Metaphysical Bicycle

The more I study physics, the more I am drawn to metaphysics.

Albert Einstein
German-born physicist

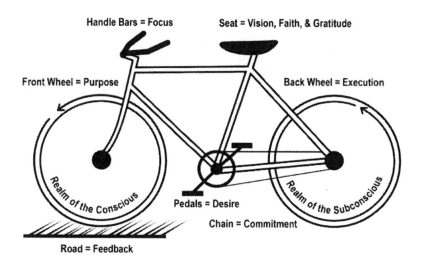

Handle Bars = Focus
Seat = Vision, Faith, & Gratitude
Front Wheel = Purpose
Back Wheel = Execution
Road = Feedback
Pedals = Desire
Chain = Commitment

You can find the entire cosmos lurking in its least remarkable objects.

Wislawa Szymborska
Polish poet

Seat = Vision, Faith, and Gratitude	Your nature, talent, energy, and essence define a vision, while stirring an impulse of something you seek. A steadiness of faith and a depth of gratitude dwell here.
Handle Bars = Focus	A natural, yet intense, concentration on what it is you want to *be*, *do*, or *have*.
Front Wheel = Purpose	A resolute aim or definite goal to be realized. Realm of the conscious mind is quartered here. The rolling wheel signifies the unwinding of one's days.
Pedals = Desire	Every push exercises your desire, defined as possibility seeking expression, as you act on an inclination with unwavering faith.
Chain = Commitment	Each revolution of the chain driving the bicycle forward is an act of commitment. Every revolution strengthens your resolve and provides a feedback loop for improvement, while memorizing the actions necessary for success. Each revolution completes a circuit of success.

Back Wheel = Execution   Action consistently directed by your purpose and driven by your desire gains traction and eventually produces results. The subconscious mind resides here. The rolling wheel symbolizes the rolling up and collecting of memories and experiences.

Road = Feedback   A winding and scenic road, now seen anew through the eyes of a more passionate life, pings back images of progress and success.

I begin to feel that myself plus the bicycle equated myself plus the world, upon whose spinning wheel we must all learn to ride, or fall into the sluiceways of oblivion and despair. That which made me succeed with the bicycle was precisely what had gained me a measure of success in life—it was the hardihood of spirit that led me to begin, the persistence of will that held me to my task, and the patience that was willing to begin again when the last stroke had failed. And so I found high moral uses in the bicycle and can commend it as a teacher without pulpit or creed. She who succeeds in gaining the mastery of the bicycle will gain the mastery of life.

Frances E. Willard
American social activist
Wheel Within a Wheel, How I Learned to Ride the Bicycle —1895

Definitions: *Life is a Bicycle—If You Stop Pedaling You'll Fall Off*

Bi-cy-cle: / 'bi-si-k l / noun (1868) the work, career or business endeavor uniquely expressing your true nature, defining principles, and foundational values, manifesting your personal best, while exhibiting your authenticity.

Bi-cy-cling: / bi-si-k ( )lin / verb (1868) the acts of performing work displaying your essence, creativity, talents, and sense of judgment, while fully engaged and alive.

Four fountainheads that stimulate your desire to discover genuine and rewarding work will be revealed. In addition, illuminating insights and enlightening questions will lead you on an evolution of thought, en route to a career or business endeavor that will satisfy your authentic purpose and bring out your absolute best.

Through two decades of contemplation and three years of research and self-reflection, I have shaped and devised what I learned into a philosophical framework. My invisible engine—which you will learn of soon enough—inspired and willed me to examine the riddle of how one goes about finding their authentic work.

Philosophy, enlightening questions, and value-identifying exercises I have learned from brilliant thinkers have been assembled and forged into *Life is a Bicycle*. The spirit of great men and women grace every page. I have done my best to add context and texture to a body of knowledge that has gone before me. I confess to the same crime as French Philosopher,

Michel de Montaigne, when he described his own work with this thought, "I have gathered a garland of other men's (and women's) flowers, and nothing is mine but the cord that binds them." You will find many quotes as you read. Consider each as a capsule of truth designed to amplify and capture the message being conveyed. A quote can instantly enlighten a reader, making a concept easier to remember in the process. Why should I endeavor to rewrite a sentence someone has already written for me?

Originality is nothing but judicious imitation.

Voltaire

French philosopher

Those who do not want to imitate anything, produce nothing.

Salvador Dali

Spanish artist

Over the course of three years, I have bicycled and performed my work as I researched and wrote this book. Three years is not really an uncommon amount of time to spend writing a book, but many would consider this slow and arduous work. However, this is one of the finer points to be conveyed—nothing feels slow and arduous when one sincerely feels they are on the right track.

Life is a Bicycle—If You Stop Pedaling You'll Fall Off is really about finding your authenticity and living a genuine life of which you can be proud. Since you spend so much of your life at work, finding your authenticity is centered on discovering the work you were elegantly engineered to perform. The American author Richard Bach said, "We teach best what we most need to learn." Finding my own authenticity was something I needed to learn. And I set out to learn this as I earnestly began writing this book in the spring of 2012.

As you read on, you are encouraged to identify and seize your unique philosophical thread, out of many woven into the fabric of this book. This will likely be a thread only you can see or feel. Upon discovery, begin at once to weave your own philosophy for success in work and life. This book contains as many formulas for success as there will be people reading it. For these reasons, you must take this information and make it your own.

One thing is certain: the alternative of not finding your peerless bi-cycle—your authentic work—will never lead to the happiness and life you were meant to live. Therefore, find and follow your genuine work. If you believe your talent, desire, energy, and appetite indicate a manner of work that is capable of bringing out your best—and this is the life you want—then let's get started.

Nature is forever beautiful and correct in principle, form, and function; even color. Rich, but rare creative souls who move and work holding-hands with Nature's creator enhance Nature's beauty. All others who do not follow their nature find life inharmonious and never as beautiful as imagined. Therefore, find and follow your nature. Work accordingly and allow the fruit and flower of your work to speak for itself—just as all of nature speaks for itself.

Ricci, don't forget to take your bicycle, you need one. It's written on the slip.

A line from the Italian movie, *The Bicycle Thief*
Directed by Vittorio De Sica/Italian director and actor

Capturing the Art of Work

Doing what you want to do is life. And there is no real satisfaction in living if you are compelled to be forever doing something which we do not like to do, and can never do what we want to do. And it is certain that you can do what you want to do. The desire to do it is the proof that you have within you the power to do it.

Wallace D. Wattles
American author

The journey of life is like a man riding a bicycle. We know he got on the bicycle and started to move. We know that at some point he will stop and get off. We know that if he stops moving and does not get off he will fall off.

William Golding
English novelist

Make your work to be in keeping with your purpose.

Leonardo da Vinci

*If a man does not keep pace with his companions, perhaps
it is because he hears a different drummer, let him step to
the music which he hears, however measured or far away.*

Thoreau

*Your work is to discover your work and then with all your
heart to give yourself to it.*

Buddha

Work cures everything.

Henri Matisse

*And those who were dancing were thought to be insane by
those who could not hear the music.*

Freidrich Nietzsche

Each man has his own vocation. The talent is the call. There is one direction in which all space is open to him. He has faculties silently inviting him thither to endless exertion.

Ralph Waldo Emerson

The master in the art of living makes little distinction between his work and his play, his labor and his leisure, his mind and his body, his information and his recreation, his love and his religion. He hardly knows which is which. He simply pursues his vision of excellence at whatever he does, leaving others to decide whether he is working or playing. To him he is always doing both.

James A. Michener
American writer

Part I

Bicycles, Love, and Keys

Let the beauty of what you love, be what you do.

Rumi
13th Century Persian Poet

Chapter 1

Blessed is he who has found his work. Let him ask no other blessing.

Thomas Carlyle
Scottish philosopher

Your Invisible Engine

The Spanish painter, Pablo Picasso, once remarked, "Life is like a train. It moves very fast, objects are hard to distinguish as you pass by them, and above all, you never get to see the engine." So, the question is lit; what is the engine? Or more precisely, what is the nature and essence of the engine driving your life? This engine rooted in your *being* engages, attracts, and energizes your *will*. It silently urges you to seek an authentic professional path which unmistakably communicates to the world "this is who I am and what I do". An impulse summons your pursuit, as your character, quietly and forever, calls you to find your best. This insatiable thirst for authenticity cannot go unquenched. Finding and following *your work* aligns your constitution with a higher calling that only you can hear. The writer's admonition to, "Look within thy heart, and write," translates to the rest of us as, "Look into thy heart and work." Therefore, turn to your heart and stake your claim. Joyfully work and connect your inward purpose with your outward ability. Be sincere with yourself, find your authenticity, and the motion of work will be as desirable as play.

Being driven to detect your work means that you possess the powers of discovery, for this is a prerequisite. Finding and reading this book is your alluring thought expressing itself into action; being faithfully obedient to that silent impulse. This is all natural and it is all very good.

The will is never free—it is always attached to an object, a purpose. It is simply the engine... it can't steer.

Joyce Cary
Irish novelist

Answering the question "What is my genuine work?" or "Who is riding my bicycle?" requires a keen sensibility and a heightened state of awareness. The train's engine, as noted by Picasso, is the heart of the locomotive, and this is a clarion clue. Understanding the heart of the matter provides the power to discover your work and reach your goals. Heart is where your true spirit lives, and the spirit of a thing is the thing. Your heart, like a locomotive's engine, creates all the power necessary. But power, no matter the magnitude, will not apply itself. Power must be recognized and appreciated; then and only then can it be useful. The power to find and follow one's most congenial work requires recognition and application.

The bicycle is a curious vehicle. Its passenger is its engine.

John Howard
Olympic cyclist

You erect your life through your work. And this work should never defy your nature. Instead it should reinforce it. Authentic work displays your power to the world, whether it is to a small audience or a full house of colleagues or customers. Ultimately, what you do depends on who you are, and who you are depends on how and what you think. Your heart—with motive and power—propels you to find and follow your work, and forever exercise to your heart's content.

Man can indeed do what he wants, but he cannot will what he wants.

Arthur Schopenhauer
German philosopher

Authentic work brings out your best. It provides for the evolution of your mind, the nourishment of your body, and the unfolding of your soul. Don't mistakenly focus on one aspect of what work offers (i.e. money) and find yourself competing for that only. The body's health may be neglected or even abused through excess or over-indulgence, but we abuse our minds and souls only by lack of nourishment. However, complete refreshment can be yours as you find and follow your work. Competing for a fraction of what truthful work has to offer is never necessary. Work truthfully and become the most highly evolved version of you possible.

Prepare yourself for an *evolution of thought* that will allow you to leap the chasm that borders a desert of toil in a job you dislike—and may even despise—into a field of endeavor uniquely suited to you. This is a place where you can actually feel yourself in your work. Rest assured that your progress and transformation need not proceed arithmetically—

in a straight line marked by the slow cadence of time—but more like a metamorphosis. Who among us could imagine the generational eons necessary for a beautiful butterfly to evolve, morph, and mutate from the caterpillar if we were ignorant of a relatively quick, natural phenomenon at play? Begin at once to shed the cocoon and discard the malaise of *inauthenticity.* Why not find and do what you *willingly want* while being thought well of it and paid well for it?

This book aligns ageless philosophical thought with practical processes of discovery by using the simple bicycle as a metaphor for work. Exercising your passion and sense of judgment will shine your genuine light, whereas performing the work of another only inks your signature on a counterfeit painting. And this creation, no matter how beautiful to others, will forever remain an empty and superfluous possession, even if your pockets are laden with gold.

I think the person who takes a job in order to live, that is to say, just for the money, has turned himself into a slave.

Joseph Campbell
American author

In the end, our work is our self-expression. The inordinate amount of time we spend at work makes it the most defining stage of our lives. As we watch a talented musician perform on his stage, it is helpful to think how fortunate it is to be gifted, and to have bravely chosen work that harmoniously exercises and displays those gifts. This epitomizes professional success—to be at work, exercising your passion and talents, doing something you love, and having an audience appreciating what you do.

I am not good in communicating with people any other way than through my work.

Henry Rollins
American musician

You were born with gifts, desires, and fascinations, and so it is you must find your destiny. Your destiny starts with answering the question, "Who is Riding My Bicycle?" There is no need to delay, so begin at once and avoid that fateful day—here before we know it—when time *just– r u n s—o u t.*

We must believe that we are gifted for something, and that this thing, at whatever cost, must be attained.

Marie Curie
Polish scientist

Rest assured, whatever your circumstances are, this work of yours will be discovered now, exactly where you find yourself. Your work is of this hour. Fate making its stand mandates that your *now* is uniquely framed for your work. Ralph Waldo Emerson said, "A true man belongs to no other time or place, but is the centre of things… insist on yourself, never imitate."

He who has done his best for his time, has lived for all times.

Friedrich Schiller
German dramatist

Every man is more than just himself, he also represents the unique, the special and always significant and remarkable point at which the world's phenomena intersect, only once in this way and never again.

Hermann Hesse
German author

Exercising your talent, passion, sense of judgment, and making a difference while doing something you love is the essence of life. There is no doubt you want to find your work, your bicycle. Not doing so creates an undercurrent of frustration. Nevertheless, so few actually succeed. Why is this so? Why don't people persevere and discover their true work? Why is the search for our life's work so often abandoned during our youth, never to be realized? We all feel the urge of the engine pointed out by Picasso. However, we are forbidden to simply turn and see it. It easily fades into the distance. Children and a rare few stubborn adults keep their dream of finding and performing at their best. This desire, like all true desires, emanates from the soul; it craves for life and will never rest unless it is fulfilled.

Oh, you weak, beautiful people who give up with such grace. What you need is someone to take hold of you— gently, with love and hand your life back to you.

Tennessee Williams
American dramatist

But if you are like most, this promising dream of riding your spectacular bicycle has been set aside somewhere along your path. Why is this so? Reasons abound. Oftentimes our daily responsibilities interfere with the goal of self-expression through work. John Lennon said: "Life is what happens while you are busy making other plans." To forgo the dream of discovering your ideal vocation forever haunts us. Ultimately, the more imperative and pressing question is, "Can your dream of discovering your work be rekindled and realized?" In the end, the answer resides in a power unique in nature—you.

We all had this priceless talent when we were young. But, as time goes by, many of us lost it.

Hans Selye
Hungarian scientist

Dreams are born in your heart and mind, and only there can they ever die.

Art Berg
American author

Chapter 2

When You Win

*Genius is nothing more or less than childhood recovered
by will, a childhood now equipped for self-expression
with an adult's capacities.*

Charles Baudelaire
French poet

*The maturity of man—that means, to have reacquired the
seriousness that one had as a child at play.*

Friedrich Nietzsche
German philosopher - Beyond Good and Evil

The quest for your unique bicycle—your life's work—pleads for an answer. Therefore, courageously listen and begin to rekindle your efforts.

Destiny finds those who listen, and fate finds the rest.

Marshall Masters
Television producer

Remain resolute through the many attempts needed to discover your work and begin cycling your unparalleled bicycle. If this were an easy task, the world's work would be conducted by happy cyclists. But is it? Just look around and you'll find the answer stamped on the world's face and revealed in its performance. Why should you ever stop your search for something so important?

Rest if you must, but don't you quit.

Iamvisionerie II Tumblr

Calvin Coolidge, the thirtieth president of the United States, claimed that the slogan "Press On" had solved and always will solve the problems of the human race, so:

Press On!!

Nothing in the world can take the place of persistence. Talent will not; nothing is more common than unsuccessful men with talent. Genius will not; unrewarded genius is almost a proverb. Education will not; the world is full of educated derelicts. Persistence and de-termination alone are omnipotent.

Searching for authentic work—the cornerstone of an authentic life—should never stop until you prevail. This high-stakes game of seek and find is not over until you win. Consider for a moment what would happen if you never found your ideal work. Now you would pass the years—one after the next—unfulfilled and disquieted; an interchangeable cog in a wheel. And what's worse, it would be someone else's wheel. Stop! Trains have engines, but they also have brakes. You are endowed with a peculiar gift, a wild card capable of trumping your history while creating your future. This is called *free will*. By its very nature, free will is a trump card that can be strategically played at any time, and at any age you choose. Freely and willingly, you continue to read.

We have to believe in free will. We've got no choice.

Isaac Bashevis Singer
Polish born Jewish author

My first act of free will shall be to believe in free will.

William James
American philosopher

Life is like a game of cards. The hand you are dealt is determinism. The way you play is free will.

Jawaharlal Nehru
Prime Minister of India

Recognize and graciously accept what it is you *will*. You have no choice other than to find your bicycle; your unique and noble work. You enjoy an essence endowed by a creative force of some kind. This essence is the one true thing upon which all else rests. It is unique to you and you alone. To discover and display one's essence is the highest art possible; always leading to a fit and proper place. To deny, refuse, or worse, rail against your innate essence always leads to an undercurrent of frustration, pain, and displeasure.

Man is the only animal that refuses to be what he is.

Albert Camus
French philosopher

It doesn't happen all at once... You become. It takes a long time. That's why it doesn't happen often to people who break easily, have sharp edges, or who have to be carefully kept... But these things don't matter at all, because once you are real you can't be ugly, except to people who don't understand... But once you are real, you can't become unreal again. It lasts for always.

Margery Williams
English author

It is our choices that show what we truly are, far more than our abilities.

J.K. Rowling
British novelist

Chapter 3

The Illustrious Bicycle

*Everyone has been made for some particular work, and
the desire for that work has been put in every heart.*

Rumi
13th Century Persian poet

The bicycle becomes the perfect metaphor for successfully exercising
your work. It symbolizes your must-find job, career, or business endeavor
that will engage your talents and energy. Broad and profound analogies
and parallels will soon become apparent to you. The bicycle—when
examined on a metaphysical plane—can help you understand, define,
and discover your work. And once this work is found, this same bicycle
will provide the components and formula for lasting success as you
exercise and work to your heart's content.

People everywhere are drawn to bicycling, making it the most
pervasive form of transportation in the world. We all know bicycling is
fun, but it can also teach us. For the purposes of this book, its teaching
will supersede its role as a mode of transportation. This transcendent
bicycle dethrones the common work routine of professional life with the
supremacy of natural law. The bicycle connects the powers of the past
with your hopes for the future. The bicycle—with its spinning wheels,
pedals, and sprockets—becomes the revolutionary vehicle that is capable
of advancing you toward your authentic work.

The overarching theme of this book is: *Life is a bicycle—if you stop pedaling, you'll fall off.* This declaration underscores a cornerstone of this book's ideology. Whether cycling along a proper professional path or not, you always need to pedal. This is true in work, play, and even retirement. If you fail to keep pedaling the bicycle, you will begin to fall off. You may recall as a child experiencing that *sinking feeling* just before impact as you fall off your bike. If you never discover your bicycle—your proper work throughout your adult life—skinned knees will be the least of your pain. You have learned and forgotten many things, but interestingly, once you learned to ride a bicycle you never forgot.

Once you have found and begun following work that is capable of nourishing your mind, body, and soul, you will never forgot it. The bicycle's universality suggests that we were born with a cycling gene embedded into our very DNA.

Do you remember when getting your first bicycle fulfilled an unforgettable childhood dream? The act of riding your new bicycle was always a dream before that first day you learned to ride. Having witnessed other children successfully riding their own bikes, you began to visualize that the act was possible and imminent. Young and unfettered, you innocently acted on a natural impulse to ride. It was a visceral wish. There was just no stopping it. Remember?

Soon your anticipation grew into reality, and through faith and single-minded purpose, a new desire fueled your action. Learning to bicycle entailed risk, and yet you surveyed the risk, felt the fear, and chose to move forward anyway. You felt destined to ride your bicycle at all costs. Your first attempts were likely weak and clumsy, but there was sincerity in your effort. Learning to bicycle took balance, and if you lost it, you instinctively adjusted to correct that imbalance.

On that bright day of your first bike ride, your thoughts about bicycling preceded the act of actually doing it. You quickly learned that mastering the art of bicycling transported you to a place you wanted to go, allowing you to do something you always wanted to do. You instantly discovered that riding your bicycle epitomized an efficient system, whereupon a particular action invariably produced a consistent result. Your thoughts led to your actions, and this made an immediate, direct demand upon your bicycle. Exerting force upon the pedals produced power and speed that was precisely equal to your demand. Your bicycle's strength grew or decreased according to the degree of force exerted. You were in complete control.

Life is like a ten-speed bicycle. Most of us have gears we never use.

Charles Schulz
American cartoonist

Getting precisely what you give is not a novel idea, but rather a universal law we are all familiar with. Humankind ultimately reaps what it sows. As a child, the bicycle transported you to your destination because you pedaled and were of service to it. You so easily put your heart into the act of bicycling that success was inevitable.

Cycling joyfully exercises a conviction of direction and firmness of purpose. Initiative, originating from within, fuels the enthusiasm necessary to maintain its forward momentum. One of the greatest attributes of bicycling is that it affords you the time to think! Yes, to cycle safely one must be aware of traffic and changing environmental conditions, but to a seasoned cyclist no conscious effort is needed. The act of thinking flourishes in this environment.

Bicycling, like proper work, faithfully exercises the body. It naturally engages the mind, and under proper conditions, beautifully inspires an unfolding soul. Bodies can be nourished and minds can be advanced, but your soul can only be unfolded and the bicycle does it all. Work encompasses thoughtful activity and physical exertion to some degree, and so it is with cycling. A cyclist harmonizes with his bicycle, becoming one with it. The bicycle is a complete system; everything is essential.

Bicycling captures individuality and exemplifies the essence of self-reliance. Your need for autonomy, which once may have atrophied, will now blossom. Unhappy, inauthentic workers are part-time slaves, but the term *slavish cyclist* appears in no lexicon on Earth. Bicycling allows for free expression and is never a machine of monotony in need of a servant. In this way, bicycling is the antithesis of forced labor. A brilliant bicycle ride never begins with a sigh of discontent.

Once you have mounted the bicycle seat, you grasp the handlebars and set a direction. The pedals, chain, and back wheel manifest your desire. They harness the energy necessary to get you somewhere. While it is possible to cycle backwards, it is much easier to cycle forward, mirroring nature's advancing style. With every symmetrical pedal stroke, a bicyclist leaves the old and enters into the new. When a bicycle is ridden long enough, it becomes a habit, and a darn good one. Bicycling is a gloriously specific action. You mount your bike knowing it will perform as imagined. Your confidence is supreme as you are certain that the bicycle will transport you to your destination.

Once you have begun cycling, your search for an extrinsic source of strength will cease to exist. Your strength and power will be magnified and become evident through the bicycle's gears and dynamics. Bicycling creates a disproportionately greater force in relation to the effort exerted.

Once you are riding a bicycle, you will be elevated from the middle of the list of the world's most efficient animals to the very top of the list, surpassing even the majestic condor. A maximum amount of work will be accomplished with only minimal effort:

Man on a bicycle can go three to four times faster than the pedestrian, but uses five times less energy in the process. Equipped with this tool, man outstrips the efficiency of not only all machines but all other animals as well... The bicycle lifted man's auto-mobility into a new order, beyond which progress is theoretically not possible...the use of the bicycle allows people to create a new relationship between their life-space and the life-time, between their territory and the pulse of their being, without destroying their inherited balance.

Ivan Illich
Austrian philosopher - Energy and Equity

Bicycling is easy. More importantly, the feeling of being productive is rewarding. Indeed, the act of gripping the handlebars will toughen your hands a bit, but it will never produce the sort of calluses that will cause you to feel nothing as you cycle to your heart's content.

Follow your bliss. I should have said follow your blisters.

Joseph Campbell
American writer

As you ride your bicycle, you will do so with joy as you cycle with a clear destination in mind. Your front wheel will be purposed in that direction. A bicycle epitomizes a final form that has remained essentially unchanged since its invention in 1868. Each push of the pedal is efficient, effective, and fun.

Think of bicycles as ride-able art that can just about save the world.

Grant Petersen
American bike designer and author

Psychologists say that the night-time dream of bicycling indicates the dreamer aspires to go someplace important, under his own power, and have fun doing it. All while maintaining a sense of balance.

Throughout history, the titans of industrialized society have wished to place and keep the proletariat (the laboring class who lack their own means of production, and hence have to sell their labor to live) beneath the Herman Hessian *wheel*. Bicycling beautifully reverses this arrangement. Cycling, like all authentic work, literally places you on a higher plane than the crushing wheel of labor. You are no longer *beneath the wheel*. Instead, you are using wheels as one of the many tools at your disposal. The authentic worker provides the heart and becomes the engine of the task, and never is this relationship reversed. Furthermore, after a sprint of cycling exertion, you can even choose to coast, while still advancing uphill for a bit.

The refusal to be a slave is really what changes the world.

Raoul Vaneigem
Belgium philosopher

There is no doubt that the act of cycling requires energy. But it never leads to exhaustion that's so severe that your leisure cannot be enjoyed. And where your workdays end with you collapsing into a haze of passivity, as you fight to muster the energy to watch television or browse the Internet.

The wheels of a bicycle easily roll in the opposite direction of a clock's sweeping hands. This is symbolic of the way that one's authentic work transcends the notion of time. An authentic cyclist never heeds the deadly tick of a monotonous clock. Yet cycling's metronomic regularity beautifully reflects the rhythm of nature. The thought of a smiling little girl jumping off her bicycle after her first successful ride, only to shout, "Boy, I never want to do that again," is hard to imagine: nor have those words ever been uttered. Ever!

On the other hand, the act of bicycling is psychologically and physically draining if you are toiling away on an uncomfortable, confining bicycle, plugging away at inauthentic work. In this instance you will find yourself ruefully scrambling to accomplish someone else's purpose and vision. By cycling in vain throughout your life—swamped in resignation and indifference—you would watch your best days pass you by, metaphorically cycling and toiling alongside Sisyphus. You probably remember learning of this tragic Greek figure who was punished with the fate of having to push a rock to the top of a mountain, whereupon the rock would roll back down. This happened again and again, each time leaving Sisyphus with the task of starting anew. Not discovering authentic work earns a fate no less absurd. There is no more dreadful punishment than futile and unrelenting labor. Sisyphus's grace occurred on his jaunt back down the mountain to fetch his beleaguered rock, as this stroll afforded him a window of reflection to consider his fate. As you join Sisyphus on his contemplative walk down the mountain, please recognize that you have many more options that weren't available to this fateful figure. You're not condemned by the gods to forever pursue pointless and disingenuous work. You have a choice. And if the *universal truth* turns out to be that all of mankind is indeed fated with the task of forever pushing a rock up a mountain, let's at least find a rock we love. If you are fated to push and follow your *rock,* you owe it to yourself to make sure that this work soulfully exhibits your essence, while fulfilling your unique and creative purpose.

In the animal kingdom, the rule is, eat or be eaten; in the human kingdom, define or be defined.

Thomas Szasz
Hungarian-born psychiatrist

Don't bend; Don't water it down; Don't edit your own soul according to fashion. Rather, follow your most intense obsessions mercilessly.

Franz Kafka
Austrian novelist

If rocks must be pushed, be sure it is a rock *you* love. Not having goals and dreams destines you to work for those who do. Venture forth demanding that you will discover your work. This is a law that supply arrives to fulfill every sincere demand. For some strange reason there is a wall—or possibly a chasm—that separates the universal demand for authentic work from its natural supply. The bicycle becomes both the vehicle and bridge, spanning a void that has existed since the beginning of time.

What can we gain by sailing to the moon if we are not able to cross the abyss that separates us from ourselves? This is the most important of all voyages of discovery.

Thomas Merton
American author

Chapter 4

The Inglorious Work Week

They were caught in the wheel from birth and they kept at it until death —and this treadmill they tried to dignify by calling it 'Life'.

Henry Miller
American writer

Masochism is a valuable job skill.

Chuck Palahniuk
American author

Finding yourself pointlessly pushing an inauthentic rock, you toil with the rather depressing goal of creating a time when you don't have to work. Arriving at the weekend is often the short-term destination, while the long-term goal is retirement.

We work to earn our leisure, and leisure has only one meaning: to get away from work, a vicious cycle.

Henri LeFebure
French philosopher and sociologist

And in between these aims you seek the oasis of *free time*. In his essay *The Abolition of Work* Bob Black explained how *free time* is only a euphemism. Bob Black said, "Our 'free time' is mostly spent, getting ready for work, going to work, returning from work, and recovering from work."

Happiness and the act of work were never meant to be antithetical or mutually exclusive. Thomas Jefferson, an excellent cyclist as a statesman, inventor, farmer, philosopher, architect, and author of the Declaration of Independence, declared for a new nation:

> *We hold these Truths to be self-evident, that all Men are created equal, that they are endowed by their Creator with certain unalienable Rights, that among these are Life, Liberty and the Pursuit of Happiness.*

BICYCLES FOR SALE
Enjoy Life, Liberty and the Pursuit of Happiness!

A *Madman's* creation, advertising the latest bicycle model, could not have painted a more alluring picture.

Creativity can solve almost any problem, the defeat of habit by originality, overcomes everything.

George Lois
American Advertising designer and executive

Life, liberty, and happiness are not ideals of leisure when real, lasting happiness can be realized by all who find and follow their work.

It is neither wealth nor splendor but tranquility and occupation which give happiness.

Thomas Jefferson

The work week customarily lasts from Monday to Friday, normally constituting five-sevenths of your week. Not enjoying your work for five straight days tends to dampen the anticipation of a fun-filled weekend. When this is the case, Sunday evenings arrive with the empty feeling of another work-week looming over you. On the other hand, once you find your bicycle, the traditional work week vanishes completely. Life grows to be true and is lived one relatively blissful day at a time. I say relatively blissful, because when you find and perform the work you love, you will still have a few rotten days here and there. It is important to be realistic. Your goal here is to find your bicycle—your authentic work—not a state of Nirvana.

Traditionally, we think of performing work in units of weeks, which brings us to an interesting observation. Examining the week as a unit of time versus the day, month, and year evidences the week as entirely man-made, and not born of natural phenomena. For example, the Earth completely rotates on its axis in a 24–hour day. You know that the length of a month is determined by the natural track of the moon, and, of course, the Earth completes an orbit of the Sun in one year. These are all units of time that are fixed by natural phenomena. But this is not true of the unit of time called the *work week*. This strange unit of time is man-made. Why is this so?

This arbitrary unit of time allows you the opportunity to anticipate and eventually receive the respite of a weekend from inharmonious activities and unfulfilling work. Consider working in a less-than-ideal job and receiving two weeks of vacation per year. Michael Ventura, American novelist and cultural critic, responded to this common experience by saying: "My employer uses 26 years of my life for every year I get to keep...And what do I get in return for my life?"

The answer is a pain-to-pleasure ratio of 26:1. But more realistically over the span of a working life, the pain-to-pleasure ratio will be 52:2, which is certainly a daunting and depressing thought. Having the good fortune of receiving four weeks of vacation per year rewards you with thirteen years of work for each precious year you gallantly call your own. Is this really society's grand bargain that you accept so willingly? There must be a better way to live a fulfilled life.

They deem me mad because I will not sell my days for gold; and I deem them mad because they think my days have a price.

Kahlil Gibran
Lebanese poet

Think! In each precious day, you will sleep for one-third and work for one-third. What then becomes of the remaining eight hours? More than likely they will be filled with basic requirements and everyday demands, and probably not chock full of joy and bliss. If you dislike your *working third*, what really do you have left?

It's a shame the only thing a man can do for eight hours a day is work. He can't eat for eight hours; He can't drink for eight hours; He can't make love for eight hours. The only thing a man can do for eight hours is work.

William Faulkner
American author

Yes, finding your work—your metaphoric bicycle—leads to an accomplished and satisfying life. This will be a true and meaningful career that satisfies your nature, power, impulse, energy, desire, talents, interest, and abilities. Ahead of you lies the best possible job, career, or business endeavor. Find and follow your work now and avoid becoming another hollow imprint fashioned by society's common stamp, forever living up to its dreadful promise.

Whoso would be a man must be a nonconformist.

Emerson
American writer - Essay on Self-Reliance

Be daring, be different, be impractical, be anything that will assist integrity of purpose, and imaginative vision against the play-it-safers, the creatures of the commonplace, the slaves of the ordinary.

Sir Cecil Beaton
English fashion, portrait and war photographer

Upon grasping the handlebars, a refreshing breeze skirts your face as you behold in your mind's eye the dream of doing your enthusiastic and professional best in a field of endeavor uniquely suited to you. You are joyfully cycling and moving to a place of importance; by your own means and under your own power. Once you begin you enjoy a sense of balance. This dream becomes reality far quicker by knowing your values and who you are than by randomly engaging in indiscriminate activities. The most lost and unproductive souls are constantly busy with extraneous activities. Action without purpose is like riding a stationary bicycle. It brings no lasting satisfaction and gets you absolutely nowhere. It has been said that not all who purposefully seek and silently wander are lost.

If you board the wrong train, it is no use running along the corridor in the other direction.

Dietrich Bonhoeffer
German theologian

Once you have become focused on finding your purposeful, value-centered work, allow the approaching exercises, principles, and timeless philosophies to place you on a path of discovery. Ageless philosophical principles, enlightening activities, and illuminating questions naturally create a confluence of confidence and conviction, all of which can ultimately lead you to success.

The bicycle's seat, handlebars, front wheel, and pedals reside in the realm of the conscious mind. The chain is the causal link to a committed, subconscious mind. However, be aware that finding your bicycle is not a guarantee. Nothing in life ever is. Risk is always present and it should be anticipated, and in some cases—even embraced.

All paths cause pain, so to choose the safe over the audacious will not give you less pain, only less beauty.

Michael Ventura
American novelist - The Zoo Where You're Fed to God

One must work and dare if one really wants to live.

Vincent van Gogh
Dutch artist

Security is mostly superstition. It does not exist in Nature, nor do the children of men as a whole experience it. Avoiding danger is no safer in the long run than outright exposure. Life is either a daring adventure or nothing.

Helen Keller

The result you obtain from engaging in the activities ahead of you will depend on your level of desire, motivation, and belief. Most importantly, your success will depend on the action you are driven to take or, more accurately, *free* yourself to take.

Always bare in mind that your own resolution to succeed is more important that any other thing.

Abraham Lincoln
U.S. president

A rewarding profession grows imminent as you practice the ideas, concepts, and philosophies to come. Relax and allow this book to drive you closer to defining and discovering your work. This will place you on a proper cycling path for the rest of your life.

Nothing is ever guaranteed, and all that came before doesn't predicate what you might do next.

Maya Lin

American artist - Designer of the Vietnam Memorial

Chapter 5

A Cycling Genius

History is full of people who successfully found work that allowed them to display the essence of their nature. It is easy to admire these quintessential bicyclists, who brilliantly illustrate the principle of discovering one's authentic work. For that reason, in this and coming chapters, we will examine some *successful bicyclists* who loved their work. Most people will feel as though it is easy to relate to these examples. However, feel free to furnish models from your own life if you find that to be helpful.

Frank Lloyd Wright—widely recognized as America's greatest architect—discovered his true work. As Frank Lloyd Wright created his architecture, he was without a doubt exercising his essence, nature, vision, and values. Frank Lloyd Wright continued to cycle and work until the very end of his life at age 93. Amazing to think that of the 1141 designs Wright conceived of—and of the 532 structures he actually built—60 percent of his production came after his 60th birthday.

He created his famous and awe-inspiring house, Fallingwater, in Mill Run, Pennsylvania, at age 61; an age when most people exercising inauthentic bicycles look forward to that mystical, revered station called retirement. Do you ever really look forward to being tired, much less *re-tired*? Hello, my friend! At 61, Frank Lloyd Wright had 32 more years of blissful, rewarding work ahead. And he would have it no other way.

Retiring is just practicing up to be dead.

Paul Harvey
American radio personality

I want to be thoroughly used up when I die. For the harder I work the more I live.

George Bernard Shaw
Irish dramatist

Frank Lloyd Wright rode such a sublime bicycle that the thought of retirement probably never occurred to him. After all, what would Frank Lloyd Wright retire from? From being himself as he designed, drew, and created hundreds of beautiful structures, using only the scant three shapes of a triangle, circle, and square as his tools?

The higher the artist, the fewer the gestures. The fewer the tools, the greater the imagination.

Ben Okri
Nigerian poet

No, this man found and followed his genuine profession. Frank Lloyd Wright was a cycling genius, and to this day he artistically communicates the ideal of discovering one's true work.

It is always interesting how the work of great artists never seems to have an end. Why is this the case, and why are so many drawn to their art? Is it possible that the artist's essence is somehow connected to the admirer's essence and therefore, their art fundamentally touches and inspires the spirit?

It is through self-knowledge that we can transform our lives into works of art.

Friedrich Nietzsche
German philosopher

As you begin to consider and contemplate your own examples of real cyclists, ask yourself: What do my examples say about me? Are they of people I admire? Do these people I hold in high esteem exemplify the best of something I have within myself? These are worthwhile questions to consider.

These bicyclists awoke to a refreshing and reinvigorating exercise they enjoyed throughout their lives. Not finding and following your distinct work deprives you of one of the greatest joys possible; the joy of creating and achieving your very best. No one is happier than the person who can't wait—on most days, at least—to get started with their work.

When I work, I relax. Doing nothing...makes me tired.

Pablo Picasso
Spanish artist

For me, not working is the real work. When I'm writing it's all the playground...

Stephen King
American novelist

Chapter 6

Two Master Keys

As you conclude the first part of this book, imagine yourself standing in front of a large control panel. See in your mind's eye a bank of flashing lights, knobs, and buttons of all sizes. Next to them are two large levers. Most people would feel mesmerized by this vast array of instrumentation. They might spend enormous amounts of time tweaking the control panel, trying to hit upon the perfect arrangement. However, the more astute will likely reach directly for the two big levers, engage them, and be done.

These two big levers on your control panel, once engaged, will propel you further and faster toward the goal of discovering your bicycle than anything else you can do. The first lever (or master key) is labeled **self-awareness**, and the second is labeled **what you think—you become**.

Though it might be tempting to fidget with all of the knobs and buttons, and each would be helpful in some form or fashion, for now just concentrate on the two big levers.

Leonardo da Vinci, Italian artist and inventor declared that, "Simplicity is the ultimate sophistication." Bicycling is certainly simple, and yet it is powerful enough to transport you to your destiny. As you read stay attentive to these two simple, yet immensely important principles. Firstly, always strive for a heightened state of self-awareness. Secondly, know that whatever you think about is what you will become. Have faith in these two principles as you are about to step onto an overpass that will transport you from where you are to where you want to be. And to complete your journey these two large levers should be fully engaged.

Become Aware

A man may be born, but to be born he must first die, and in order to die, he must first awake.

Carl Sandburg
American poet

To initiate the task of becoming more aware, it is important to begin with the awareness that you will have to start from where you are. That is, you must start from wherever you reside on the self-awareness continuum. Therefore, commence this exercise by utilizing the highest degree of self-awareness you can marshal, coupled with the supreme belief that an ever-higher grade of self-awareness is accessible; because it is. Many people possess self-awareness, having acquired the habit of living in the moment. If that is the case for you, keep in mind the value of reviewing this concept. However, most people will find this to be new and enlightening information.

The present moment is the instant of your destiny, and it all starts with a choice, your choice.

Guy Finley
American author

Developing self-awareness begins with self-examination on the physical plane. Improved self-awareness on the physical plane augments self-awareness on the mental and psychological planes. Improved self-awareness allows you to feel your engine's essence, being, nature, and will, with all roads pointing toward the discovery of your true work.

If it is reason which makes man, it is feeling which guides him.

Jean-Jacques Rousseau
Genevan philosopher

Starting where you are—as you are holding this book—casually and non-critically observe your physical self. How are you sitting? Is your head relaxed or are you straining your neck at an unnatural angle? Notice the position of your hands—are muscles being applied unnecessarily? Did you just now reposition your body to be more comfortable? Now use your mind's eye to see your face. Do you have a tense expression or are you using muscles unnecessarily? Did you choose to relax your face? Try smiling. Can you see yourself smiling?

The aim in Life is to live and to live means to be aware. Joyously, drunkenly, serenely, divinely, aware.

Henry Miller
American writer

When one realizes one is asleep, at that moment one is already half-awake.

P. D. Ouspensky
Russian philosopher

Higher levels of self-awareness, once experienced, can be exercised at will. Awareness equals control, so it is worthwhile to choose to change and be in charge of yourself. In addition, improving your self-awareness enhances your discernment of others regarding their attitudes. This allows you to understand if their motives are benevolent or unkind. As you work through these basic facial awareness exercises, notice how your overall awareness increases. This noticeable progress occurred in just the last few minutes. Imagine what more time and attention could bring about, as this radiant iceberg floats into view. As you sense increased physical self-awareness, know that the same process can be directed toward the realm of your heart and mind. This is where the pistons of Picasso's never-to-be-seen engine perform their deeds.

The mind's first step to self-awareness must be through the body.

George A. Sheehan
American writer

Now prepare to take a leap in awareness from the physical plane into the realm of your thoughts and emotions. Imagine yourself standing to your side and observe your mental and emotional self. Be sure to do so without judgment or criticism. Observe whatever you are concerned or happy about from this new vantage point. Observe your mental revelations as if watching a falling star crossing the sky. Simply observe yourself as you stand with your arm around the shoulders of your exhausted Greek friend, Sisyphus, near the bottom of a mountain of work. Just as assuredly as Sisyphus senses the weight of his fate, you should experience the elation that accompanies a higher state of awareness.

An exasperated Sisyphus knows his truth but is powerless to change it. However, you can change your fate. A higher state of awareness is one essential master key needed to unlock the door leading to your true work. This is work that will be grounded in your truth and values, which serve as the fuel for Picasso's never-to-be-seen engine.

The American author Guy Finley has said the following about the topic of awareness:

> *Before you can change the course of your destiny, you must first gain access to that secret place within yourself where your own future is being created moment by moment. Yes, there is such a location. It's real. And yes, you can learn to dwell there and direct your destiny. This truly timeless place—where all of your life-choices are made for you—is what we understand, in concept, as the Present Moment. The Present Moment is actually a Cosmic Seed of a sort from out of which springs all that comes later. The Present Moment is where our Being—which is a timeless unconditioned Energy—meets and animates our Nature. Now our Nature, on the other hand, lives only in time; meaning it's fabricated from all or our past experiences. Said slightly differently, our nature is a psychological body of memories and knowledge structured by our social, economic, and religious conditioning. The Present Moment, where our Being and Nature meet, is the instant of our destiny. And up until now, we've had little real choice in how our fates unfold, because it's always been our*

nature, our accumulated past with all of its fears, compulsions, and doubts that has been running the show. The third force, that can be at your command as a kind of special window into the Present Moment is called Awareness. Your awareness of the Present Moment is the Present Moment.

It will be in the *now* of a present moment that your work will be discovered. Granted, faith and action are necessary. It was not so long ago that you held the desire, harnessed the faith, and attempted your very first bicycle ride. Did it work?

It is easier to perceive error than to find truth, for the former lies on the surface and is easily seen, while the latter lies in the depth, where few are willing to search for it.

Johann Wolfgang von Goethe
German philosopher

The work of raising your self-awareness is the work of a lifetime. Therefore, strive to be fully aware in the present moments of your life every chance you can. Observing yourself watch television is another simple exercise you can try. If you begin to notice everyday colors as more brilliant and the edges of objects appearing sharper, you'll know you're making progress.

When you're in the yard talking to three guys, see four.
See yourself. Dig yourself.

Mafia Capo's third proposition for serving jail-time

As you begin to sense emotions and thoughts passing through your heart and mind, observe them and ask yourself, "Did you feel that? Did you think that? Why are you feeling and thinking that? Wasn't that interesting?" Don't be judgmental in your self-observation. Simply observe and make mental notes as you begin penning your thoughts for later review[1].

Be inquisitive of what your heart and mind wish to divulge, as only the curious have something to find. Your heart is the engine of your being. Allow it to ignite a torch that illuminates the path to your true and noble work. In this way your heart can supersede your mind, paving your authentic path.

Finding the work you love is not a cerebral process. Listen
to your own heart and learn to trust what it is saying.
While your heart knows, your head can only suppose.

Laurence G. Boldt
American author

---

1   At this time it will be important for you to begin a personal and confidential journal as you advance through this and other exercises. A note captures fleeting but important insights coming uniquely to you and you alone. Act now and your journal will reap benefits beyond belief.
The palest ink, trumps the strongest memory. ~ Chinese Proverb

Consciously strive to be alive and aware in this present moment of your life. Let's face it: *if you are to live your dreams, you must first wake up!*

The gent who wakes up and finds himself a success hasn't been asleep.

Wilson Mizner
American dramatist

The author Tom Robbins wished for his audience to awaken when he described this state of affairs:

> You've heard of people calling in sick. But have you ever thought about calling in well? It'd go like this: you get the boss on the line and say, 'Listen, I've been sick ever since I started working here; but today, I'm well and I won't be in anymore.' Call in well.

You may think what a preposterous, even shocking consideration, but as the Armenian philosopher, George Gurdjieff, explained:

> All people are asleep. And in order to awaken them from their stupor long enough to introduce them to a new idea or way of doing things, you must give them some sort of conscious shock.

What You Think—You Become

What you think—you become. This captions the second large lever on your control panel of life. In the preamble of *As a Man Thinketh*, James Allen may have explained this best when he wrote that his book:

...stimulates men and women to the discovery and perception of the truth that, 'They themselves are makers of themselves' by virtue of the thoughts which they choose and encourage; that mind is the master-weaver, both of the inner garment of character and the outer garment of circumstance—and that, as they may have hitherto woven in ignorance and pain they may now weave in enlightenment and happiness...'

In addition, James Allen adds:

The plant springs from, and could not be without, the seed. So every act of man springs from the hidden seeds of thought, and could not have appeared without them... Act is the blossom of thought, and joy and suffering are its fruit. Man is made and unmade by himself.

So the second master key principle to employ is **what you think—you become.** The self-help and motivational speaker Brian Tracy says, "You are not what you think you are. But what you think, you are."

As a man thinketh in his heart, so he is.

Proverbs 23:7

The words you place behind the very powerful "*I am...*" dictate your vocation and ad-vocation. Your thoughts are the genesis of your actions; make no mistake.

The first moon mission is one example of an inspired thought that was followed by monumental action. Do you think this historic moment was possible because a NASA scientist suddenly looked around and said, "Look, we've invented all this stuff. Let's go to the moon?" Not hardly. The thought of traveling to the moon and back was first proposed by President Kennedy. Kennedy's thought, animated with passion and conviction, was the catalyst that galvanized engineers and placed vast resources in motion. This in turn led to the construction of all the gear necessary to make a successful voyage to the moon and back. Understand this critical idea—your thoughts precede all action.

Let a man radically alter his thoughts, and he will be astonished at the rapid transformation it will effect in the material conditions of his Life. Men imagine that thought can be kept secret, but it cannot. It rapidly crystallizes into habit, and habit solidifies into circumstance.

James Allen
English philosopher

To conclude, the control panel that's always at the ready has flashing lights, knobs, and switches. But the two most important levers constantly at your command are:

☐ **Become more self-aware**

☐ **What you think, you become.**

The art of being wise is the art of knowing what to overlook.

William James
American philosopher

Now, with these keys in hand, you're psychologically equipped to begin a rewarding journey through your own evolution of thought. Find your truth within, for you alone harness the power to make it so. It is true understanding, and not simply knowledge, that increases your capacity to work and live according to your nature.

Doubt is the vestibule which all must pass before they can enter the temple of wisdom. When we are in doubt and puzzle out the truth by our own exertions, we have gained something that will stay by us and serve us again. But, to avoid the trouble of the search we avail ourselves of the superior information of a friend, such knowledge will not remain with us; we have not bought, but borrowed it.

Charles Caleb Colton
English writer

See yourself as you truly are, and not only as others see you. You were designed with the inalienable right to be free—to be yourself. Lasting freedom comes when you work according to your nature, and never based on the nature imposed by others. Once your work is found, it is easy to be dedicated to it. Ultimately, it is in your nature to be dedicated to your work. There is no freer human being than one who works according to his nature. Your mind can only do one thing—form ideas—and professionally you want to be paid for your ideas. It is only when your ideas start to make some noise that you can be compensated. When your professional actions display and objectify your essence, nature, and will, personal freedom is sure to follow.

Anticipation turns into actualization as you exercise your beautiful bicycle. Concentrated thought evolves into action and in time you find yourself performing work you can't imagine going through life without. As you ride your bicycle, every enthusiastic push of the pedal takes work—a lot of work—and this is your work.

As you continue to read, if you sincerely feel naturally attracted to these ideas, know that you are making a mental, emotional, and heavy cycling-stroke in the right direction.

Why, here under our noses, is the greatest of all motive powers. Why human thought is a real element, a real force, darting out like electricity from every man's and woman's mind, injuring or relieving, killing or curing, building fortunes or tearing them down, working for good or ill, every moment, night and day, asleep or awake, carving, moulding(sic) and shaping people's faces and making them ugly or agreeable.

Prentice Mulford
American author - Thoughts are Things

Dreams pass into the reality of action. From the actions stems the dream again; and this interdependence produces the highest form of living.

Anais Nin
French-born author

Part II

Why Find Your Bicycle?

*There is no craving or demand of the human mind
more constant and insatiable than that for exercise and
employment and the desire seems the foundation of most
of our passions and pursuits.*

David Hume
Scottish philosopher

*If a man loves the labour of his trade, apart from any
question of success or fame, then gods have called him.*

Robert Louis Stevenson
Scottish writer

*All men should strive to learn before they die, what they
are running from, and to, and why.*

James Thurber
American cartoonist & author

To be yourself is the greatest privilege of life.

Thomas Carlyle
Scottish philosopher

Chapter 7

Introduction

When one is engaged in a favorite pursuit or a subject absorbingly interesting, the normal conception of labor or time and artificial social distinctions disappear from the mind. In fact, life itself is absorbed in the engagement, or it may be said that one's life is turned in harmony with eternal life.

Gunji Koizumi
Master of Judo

Discovering one's work takes initiative, time, and energy—and yet you are driven to pursue. Why? By asking the question, "Why not pursue my authentic work?" you very quickly see there is only one direction home. This desire to find your true work is your *spirited will* wishing to fulfill its true purpose. And it is certain you have a purpose. Your professional authenticity is grounded in who and what you are. Who and what you are—and more importantly, what you are to become—depends on what you think. The act of thinking ancestors all of what you do. You already know, or should strive to learn very quickly, that your thoughts are causes and your work and results are the effects. And within this truth lies the caveat which ensnares society and leads its members to settle for and live a life of uninspired, disingenuous work.

Your thoughts—through no fault of your own—have been shaped and bent by society's pliers. This result comes from your environment, government, parents, teachers, and all other social influences that have shaped you, right up to this very moment. It is indisputable that each of these dynamics has played a heavy hand in determining exactly who you are today. These conditioned and influenced thoughts have led you to the space you occupy in life—what it is you do, and have always done, for work and play. There was never a choice really. Personal action follows thought as directly and assuredly as winter follows fall.

Your escape from this vicious cycle of conditioned thinking requires your willingness to feel and listen to your *will*. Your *will* is the inner impulse that Picasso described as the engine you never get to see. However, by building a heightened state of awareness, you can begin to feel the strength and energy of your *will*. Learning to listen to your *will* and what it loves—and then translating what you hear into a practical formula for action—is the only path to authenticity.

There is a soul at the centre of nature, and over the will of every man, so that none of us can wrong the universe.

Ralph Waldo Emerson
American writer - Essay on Spiritual Laws

Will and *love* are twin sisters pointing you in the direction of your *true north*. Become faithful to your *will* and what it loves. Allow it to overwhelm your conditioned thinking. Only then can you shear the orbit of conditioned thinking and the conditioned doing that is sure to follow. You are taking a heavy step forward as you get your head around this idea. The act of taking this first step of understanding is essential before you can successfully push that first pedal stroke into the cycling adventure that lies before you.

One's *will* exists on a higher spiritual plane than one's conditioned thinking. Your *will's* desire is revealed by way of four marvelous and universal fountainheads. While it is possible for these fountainheads' originating headwaters to be disregarded easily, their effervescent current can never be completely impeded. The Roman Emperor, Marcus Aurelius said, "Look within. Within is the fountain of good, and it will ever bubble up, if you will ever dig."

Understanding and appreciating these four universal fountainheads— whose waters flow not from historical and conditioned thought, but from your spiritually inspired *will*—allows you the chance to shoot the gap of inauthentic work. This is a gap that has always existed between true *will* and *love*, and what we are conditioned to think and do.

Man can indeed do what he wants, but he cannot will what he wants.

Arthur Schopenhauer
German philosopher

What I love is not my will, but above it.

Ralph Waldo Emerson
American writer

Never finding and following your genuine work is like spending your life in a poorly lit prison cell, with the door not only unlocked, but visibly open. Of course, you'll sense an underlying urge to escape, but strangely your desire isn't strong enough to do so. Having heard of or read about one or two escapees offers no consolation and is certainly no psychological match for an imprisoned society whose examples are overwhelming at every turn. As a member of society's coterie of everyday prisoners, you experience your fair share of temporal gratifications. Everything is so normal that you become convinced that all must be well for you also. However, this vacuous enjoyment—no matter how immediately satisfying—will inevitably morph and twist into emptiness at best, and pain at worst. This is your fate if you never find your work.

Darkness abounds in this cell of self-incarceration. In periodic moments of intense personal reflection, you may attempt to make sense of the darkness by flooding it with light. But this is an ironically impossible proposition. Yet the strong will try again and again—and good for them. Your natural default to fight this darkness is to do what society has taught you. You work at something—anything. Wishing to maintain some semblance of light, you feverishly work to keep a host of small oil lamps lit, by whatever means necessary. The task of keeping your meager lamps lit against this vast darkness causes an undercurrent of exasperation. Finally, in a fit of frustration, you strike your fist against the prison wall, and to your surprise a crack appears. Suddenly, a hole opens up and a piercing light pours through. And in this light there is an answer. You don't need more oil lamps to keep you busy. You need more holes. Immediately inspired, you continue to thrash against the prison walls, creating larger holes until the entire infrastructure of the cell begins to fall away. And even though the door has always been open, you now escape through a self-created gap. Your understanding of how it was that you first came to be imprisoned provides you with confidence to exit now. It had to be this way. You finally feel like all is well.

Four fountainheads (originating springs or origins) expose and illuminate your *will*, which is forever doing its best to drive you in the direction of your genuine work. A rare few will act on the impulses that emanate from one or more of these fountainheads. But most will not, instead feeling defeated, resigned, or surprisingly uninterested. However, these four fountainheads are forever forging a desire that exhorts you to seek, define, and follow your distinctive work. Refusing to act on at least one of these four origins of desire keeps you locked in a dim prison cell of *inauthenticity*.

People are strange: they are constantly angered by trivial things, but on a major matter like totally wasting their lives, they hardly seem to notice.

Charles Bukowski
American writer

Chapter 8

Four Fountainheads Reveal and Spur Your Desire, Will and Love

One can survive in only one of two ways—By the independent work of his own mind or as a parasite fed by the mind of another.

Ayn Rand
Russian born writer and philosopher

The headwaters of these four fountainheads provide the fuel of your invisible engine. They forever flame the psychological torches that light the way to your genuine work. They are:

1. **Intuition**: To be heard

2. **Creativity**: To be explored

3. **Growth**: To be enjoyed

4. **Dreams**: To be appreciated

A man lives by believing something; not by debating and arguing about many things.

Thomas Carlyle
Scottish philosopher

Before you begin investigating the reasoning behind your need to discover your work, know that you will have one critical ally—time.

Time is the wisest of all counselors.

Plutarch
Greek historian

Time is the cosmic fabric upon which everyone's life story is woven. And nature—in its brilliance—has forged a judicious pact with its citizenry by ensuring that each day; all are awarded the exact same measure of time: 24 hours. And no one—prince or pauper, saint or thief—can bargain for or steal a minute more, nor forgo a minute less. The productive and the non-productive each have 24 hours in a day. You are as rich as anyone when it comes to the currency of time. Whatever you choose to do, you will cycle, work, and rest on the level and fair playing field of time.

Time is the coin of your life. It is the only coin you have, and only you can determine how it will be spent. Be careful lest you let people spend it for you.

Carl Sandburg
American poet

Do you fear that you are too old to find rewarding and satisfying work? At this very second, you are the youngest you will be for the rest of your natural life. Therefore, go do something youthful and fun—as you read these words you are young as you will ever be: now you are older, and now older still.

The more sand has escaped from the hourglass of our life, the clearer we should see through it.

Niccolo Machiavelli
Italian historian & philosopher

Maybe you are just too busy to find your work? According to Henry David Thoreau, "It is not enough to be busy, so are the ants. The question is what are you busy about?"

Of course, you are a busy person. There must be something good on television, and a new game to be played on your phone awaits your attention. The sound you hear is a shot across your bow awakening you to the adventure of finding out who is riding your bicycle. After all, this will be a quest that will allow you the opportunity to once and for all exit society's orbit of uninspired work.

The power which resides in him is new in nature, and none but he knows that which he can do, nor does he know until he has tried.

Ralph Waldo Emerson
American writer

Let's explore the four universal fountainheads sourcing the emotions of desire, will, and love, flowing through us all. These are the genesis of authentic work. They serve as the very first guideposts to discovering one's professional bliss.

Chapter 9

Intuition: To Be Heard

The more and more each is impelled by that which is intuitive, or relying upon the soul force within, the greater, the farther, the deeper, the broader, the more constructive may be the result.

Edgar Cayce

American mystic

The intuitive mind is a sacred gift and the rational mind is a faithful servant. We have created a society that honors the servant and has forgotten the gift.

Albert Einstein

German-born physicist

Having your hidden thoughts revealed through your work is the highest form of art possible. Baruch Spinoza, the Dutch philosopher, was well-versed in this skill. He worked as a lens grinder by day and as a writer by night. It was Spinoza who proposed that there are three degrees of knowledge available to you. The first, which Spinoza considered to be the lowest degree of knowledge, was derived from everyday base stimuli you might encounter in your life. For example, you might feel your hand on something hot and immediately remove it. Spinoza's second and more advanced level of knowledge, he labeled Reason and Logic. This second level of knowledge occurred when various people observed the same traits or consistencies in an object or phenomena and agreed on what they saw. The third, and in his mind highest degree of knowledge, was that of Intuition. He said when you had moments or flashes of intuition you were seeing "God's Thoughts". The English poet, Robert Graves amplified this point when he said, "Intuition is the supra-logic that cuts out all the routine processes of thought and leaps straight from the problem to the answer."

Intuition will tell the thinking mind where to look next.

Jonas Salk
American Medical researcher

Therefore, intuition is your first fountainhead of paramount importance. For many, the idea of sincerely listening inward, by consciously paying attention to a thought or image flashing into one's mind, can be very difficult. After all, these are your thoughts and they come easily and unexpectedly. Your question may be, "Why take it seriously? It's just me, and what do I know? Who am I to have the audacity to listen to or believe in these fleeting moments of intuition?" Many of us developed this type of self-defeating mindset from the very people who loved us the most.

All children are born geniuses but only a few make it through.

Walt Disney
American businessman

Just listening to your intuition takes nerve. It also requires a revolutionary thought to act on your intuitions. It is interesting how, as time passes, our personal value is derived from all the material things we have collected—our house, title, cars, bank account, and so on. In order to actually hear, feel, and act on our intuition, it becomes necessary to make a paradigm shift toward understanding that the most valuable aspects of life are found within.

A man's true state of power and riches is to be in himself.

Henry Ward Beecher
American clergyman

When we discover that the truth is already in us, we are all at once our original selves.

Dogen Zenji
Zen Buddhist teacher

In his book *Psycho-Pictography*, author Vernon Howard describes the idea of listening to yourself and believing in what you hear this way:

A Swiss Shepherd boy was kidnapped by passing gypsies. As he was hustled away inside the wagon, he heard the ringing of the village bell. The sound become fainter and fainter as the wagon carried him away. But the bell's special tone made a permanent impression upon his mind. Years later, as he grew up, the memory of that bell stirred a restless urge within. It made him weary of the gypsy life. He longed to return to his rightful home. So he broke away from the gypsy camp and began his search. He wandered from country to country, village to village, listening intensely for the special ring of that single bell. He heard many peals as he journeyed along, but he always detected a false ring, and so refused to be lured away. Finally, while pausing by the roadside to rest, he heard a faintly familiar peal. He turned in its direction. The farther he walked, the more swiftly he stepped. Something within him knew that he was hearing his village bell at last. And he followed it all the way home. Likewise, the ring of truth is inside every man and woman. And this is not something merely mystical or philosophical. It is a practical fact. If a man learns to listen, if he refuses to be lured away by false sounds, he will find his way home. The ring of truth will always be recognized by the man who listens. And every man has the capacity to listen and to follow.

The art of listening and following your intuition may seem easy. However, it is far easier not to do so. At some point in the past, you or someone who loved you took the time and spent the money to buy a bicycle for you. You could never be satisfied having to borrow a friend's bicycle time and time again.

You deserve to find proper work and a congenial place. You have been created from the same source as any amazing person you have ever envied or admired. Your inimitable energy—wishing to burn as brightly as any star—was created to fulfill a purpose. That purpose can only be accomplished through sincere work.

I have tried to do what is true and not ideal.

Henri de Toulouse Lautrec

French artist

*Success means having the courage, the determination,
and the will to become the person you believe you
were meant to be.*

George A. Sheehan
American writer

You have talents and appetites like no other, and there must be a reason why. Your unique place in space and time means you are to perform your work in your own way. This chance only comes *once*. As you continue to read and do the exercises in this book, don't forget about your chief ally—time. Because the good news is that your unique place in space and time—your *once*—will more than likely last for decades. You will have plenty of time to fail, again and again, if necessary; yet you will also have plenty of time to succeed. Failure plus persistence is a true formula for success. The restaurateur, Truett Cathy said, "It may take time, sometimes a lot of time, to be successful. But it takes a lifetime to fail."

*If a man is not faithful to his own individuality, he cannot
be loyal to anything.*

Claude McKay
Jamaican-American writer

*May I be I, is the only prayer—not may I be great or good
or beautiful, or wise or strong.*

E.E. Cummings
American writer

Chapter 10

Creativity: To Be Explored

Among Human Beings, creativity is a natural, not an exceptional trait. Birds fly, fish swim and humans create.

Laurence Boldt
American author - Be, Do and Have Anything

Whoever undertakes to create soon finds himself engaged in creating himself.

Harold Rosenberg
American writer

The second fountainhead that is continually stimulating your desire and animating your will is your creativity. This natural creativity demands an outlet. The channels of release for this creativity come through either work or play. Now it's possible you already feel you're pretty creative, while others, understandably, may not.

Show me what you do, and I will know you.

William Blake
English poet

It's a creative celestial energy that forces the beautiful flower from its green stem. Creativity abounds in nature. We see its work in landscapes, mountains, and striking oceans. All of these are the work of some creative hand. It is not a great leap of faith to believe that this creative hand's most intelligent beings would be imbued with this same creative impulse.

Inside you there's an artist you don't know about.

Auguste Rodin
French sculptor

What would it profit thee to be the first of echoes?

Frederick Tennyson
English poet

No commercially successful creator, like your favorite writer, sculptor, painter, or musician, ever diminishes the truth that we are all indeed creative beings. At the end of the day, we are the ultimate creators of ourselves.

We are all self-made, only the rich will admit it.

Jimmy Durante
American comedian

Creativity's cosmic stage is the work you choose. Creativity flows in the same way that we should bicycle—easily and unobstructed. And this idea of an active flow of creativity is mirrored in nature, which is the universal watermark that indicates a principle is indeed correct. Nature's creative flow gives us blowing winds, shining suns, and flowing rivers. Likewise, rolling wheels, spinning pedals and the world's work should express our creativity to some degree.

The deleterious effects that result from the hindrance of creative flow are also seen in nature. The Dead Sea is dead because it has no outlet in which to flow. This causes its salinity to rise to ten times the level found in the bountiful oceans. A beautiful bicyclist who has cloistered himself in self-erected walls—with no open road to display his creativity—will always dread the coming workday.

> *When I am, as it were, completely myself, entirely alone, and of good cheer... that ideas flow best and most abundantly.*

Wolfgang Amadeus Mozart
Austrian musician

Emerson said, "When Nature has work to be done, she creates a genius to do it."

> *Genius does what it must, and talent does what it can.*

Robert Bulwer-Lytton
English statesman and poet

Nature's fountainheads, as a genius has designed them, are pushing you to follow your own nature by discovering your authentic work. Your goal today is to discover that work. Don't stifle your creative impulse any longer, no matter how faint it is. Be decisive in knowing that you can find and follow your proper path. The habit of stifling an impulse is your conditioned thinking, bent by society's stamp, doing its habitual best to maintain its dominance. According to the psychologist William James, "There is no more miserable human being than one in whom nothing is habitual but indecision."

The universe hands you opportunities for a while, and if you don't take them, the universe says to itself, 'Oh, I see, this person doesn't like opportunities' and stops giving them to you.

Doug Coupland

Canadian novelist

It is important to view yourself as the co-creator that you really are, graciously holding hands with some form of supreme intelligence. The American psychologist, Abraham Maslow said, "Individual, personal freedom and self-fulfillment deepens upon the conscious expansion of your innate creative capacities. Without such expression, you would meet with unhappiness and unnecessary limitation."

There is talent, there is genius, then there is the divine.

Gregory Corso

American poet - Explaining the trajectory of creative achievement

Finally, it is important to never fret over the idea that your work just seems frivolous. This reaction is another symptom of society's misguided and manufactured traps. Just because what you aspire to do is easy, interesting, and fun does not debase its value; neither does it negate the loftiness of the work necessary to accomplish it. Your desire to perform uniquely assigned work is the sextant of the soul, aligning your constitution with that of a grand cosmos. Your work emanates from your essential nature. As you follow your unique path, a sense of joy prevails.

Creation is a drug I can't do without.

Cecil B. DeMille
American film director and producer

The merit of originality is not novelty; it is sincerity. The believing man is the original man; He believes for himself, not for another.

Thomas Carlyle
Scottish philosopher

Chapter 11

Growth: To Be Enjoyed

If you are not a-busy being born you are a-busy dying.

Bob Dylan
American singer & songwriter

Life is occupied in both perpetuating itself and in surpassing itself; if all it does is maintain itself, then living is only not dying.

Simone de Beauvoir
French writer

The third fountainhead stimulating your *will* and driving you to ascertain your authentic work comes from your desire for growth. This applies across all planes: mental, physical, emotional, and spiritual. Growth equals change, and we know change is constant in our lives. Growth can be generative or degenerative, but either way it is going to be. How it impacts us depends on what we think and do. Listen, feel, and follow your unique fountainhead of growth to direct your thoughts, mold your actions, and dictate your fate.

Change and growth take place when a person has risked himself and dares to become involved with experimenting with his own life.

Herbert Otto

German general

Always strive to grow, or suffer the consequences of stagnation. This is a very simple and exacting formula. Any effort to hinder growth will lead to a slow death by a thousand paper cuts: incremental disaster at its excruciating best.

The true tragedy in life is not death, but what we let die inside of us while we live.

Norman Cousins

American author

Once again, it is helpful to turn toward nature as your eternal teacher. A lifetime spent running in opposition to nature's lessons will surely place you on a wayward path. Nature is the classroom of the universe's spiritual laws. Therefore, it bodes well to remain mindful of nature's lessons. If nature is not the one to teach the universe's principles and laws, what is? For instance, nature wants its citizens to live a generous and lavish life because nature is the mirror. As a case in point, consider that one seed grows into a plant which in time will produce hundreds of seeds, each containing the magical ability to grow. In turn, those hundreds of seeds are governed by some supreme force that mandates millions more will be created.

Yes, there is no doubt that nature displays a lavishness that borders on wasteful. Therefore, embrace growth and become instantly aligned with nature. Aspire to work as nature works, and as Emerson said, "move at its pace." To find your blissful work, you have to become aligned with the physical and metaphysical laws of nature's universal intelligence. One is most aligned with nature when seeking and embracing personal growth.

When they tell you to grow up, they mean stop growing.

Tom Robbins
American author

To exist is to change, to change is to mature, to mature is to go on creating oneself endlessly.

Henri Bergson
French philosopher

Chapter 12

Dreams: To Be Appreciated

One day it will have to be officially admitted that what we have christened reality is an even greater illusion than the world of dreams.

Salvador Dali
Spanish Surrealist painter

The future belongs to those who believe in the beauty of their dreams.

Eleanor Roosevelt
First Lady

The fourth and final fountainhead that stimulates your *will* and drives you to find your legitimate professional endeavor comes from a capacity to dream. Dreaming is the ultimate act of what has been coined as "going into the silence." Dreams are windows that create a direct portal into your true self. They act as your private screening room, projecting what can be your life and its work. Dreams are as close as you get to actually seeing your engine, which was described by Picasso as un-seeable. The French philosopher Michel de Montaigne said, "I believe it to be true that dreams are the true interpreters of our inclinations."

*The greatest achievement was at first and for a time
a dream.*

James Allen
British philosopher

In *As a Man Thinketh*, James Allen wrote:

> *The oak sleeps in the acorn; the bird waits in the egg. And in
> the highest vision of a soul a waking (angel) stirs. Dreams are the
> seedlings of realities. Your circumstances may be uncongenial, but
> they shall not remain so if you only perceive an ideal and strive
> to reach it. You can't travel within and stand still without. Here
> is a youth hard pressed by poverty and labor. Confined long hours
> in an unhealthy workshop; unschooled and lacking all the arts of
> refinement. But he <u>dreams</u> of better things. He thinks of intelligence,
> or refinement, of grace and beauty. He conceives of, mentally builds
> up, an ideal condition of life. The wider liberty and a larger scope
> takes possession of him; unrest urges him to action, and he uses all
> his spare times and means to development of his latent powers and
> resources. Very soon so altered has his mind become that the workshop
> can no longer hold him. It has become so out of harmony with his
> mind-set that it falls out of his life as a garment is cast aside. And
> with the growth of opportunities that fit the scope of his expanding
> powers, he passes out of it altogether. Years later we see this youth as a
> grown man. We find him a master of certain forces of the mind that
> he wields with worldwide influence and almost unequaled power. In
> his hands he holds the cords of gigantic responsibilities....*

So, what do you dream of? And more importantly, what do your
dreams mean? After all, they must mean something. Dreams underpin

the conviction necessary to take action on your behalf. Your present state of affairs is an accumulation of your dreams and the action—or lack thereof—that followed them. In addition, dreaming brings out latent powers that exist inside the dreamer. The greatest progress known to mankind is the result of the dreamers of this world. If you were to take the dreamers out of the history books, who would care to read them?

If there were dreams to sell, what would you buy?

Thomas Lowell Beddoes
English poet

For the more truly he consults his own powers, the more difference will his work exhibit from the work of any other. His ambition is exactly proportioned to his powers.

Ralph Waldo Emerson
American writer - Essay on Spiritual Laws

Daydreaming has often been characterized as a sign that desire exceeds what you truly believe is possible for yourself. However, the real role of dreams is to foreshadow upcoming events. This is true since nothing that has been spiritually inspired can remain meaningless. Your capacity to dream signifies an expectation that there are better things to come. Yet this ability can be abused if one's dreams are never acted upon with force and vigor. Above all, never discourage your propensity and capacity to dream.

*Whether or not the philosophers care to admit that we
have a soul, it seems obvious that we are equipped with
something or other which generates dreams and ideals
and which sets up values.*

John Erskine
American educator & writer

*Dreaming is an act of pure imagination, attesting in
all men a creative power, which, if it were available in
waking, would make every man a Dante or Shakespeare.*

H. F. Hedge
British philosopher

*After your first day of cycling, one dream is inevitable.
A memory of motion lingers in the muscles of your
legs, and round and round they seem to go. You ride
through dreamland on wonderful dream bicycles that
change and grow.*

H. G. Wells
English writer

From the four fountainheads of intuition, creativity, growth, and
dreams flows the essence of your *desire, will, and love.* Each fountainhead
is impelling you toward authentic work. There are people who choose to
listen to these fountainheads and obey them. On the other hand, there
are others who strangely spend a precious lifetime in painful avoidance.

These fountainheads will provoke you to pursue your ideal work if you listen carefully. Be appreciative of their wisdom because now—perhaps for the very first time—you are beginning to feel the vibration of your engine's will. Your desire to seek your best has a unique genesis, proving that your work is to be unique. Furthermore, your desire to discover dignified and joyful work proves that you have the ability to find it.

Your reasons for performing your best are ever-present. This is a natural inclination; as natural as riding your first bicycle. Read on and stake your claim.

If you do what you like, you never really work. Your work is your play.

Hans Seyle
Hungarian scientist

I was not looking for my dreams to interpret my life, but rather for my life to interpret my dreams.

Susan Sontag
American author

*You know you have found your work if you are happy...
Profound joy of heart is like a magnet that indicates the
path of your Life. One has to follow it even though one
enters into a way full of difficulties.*

Mother Teresa
Roman Catholic sister

Chapter 13

The Magical Classified Employment Ad

You will cycle an authentic or inauthentic bicycle every working day of your life. And you will either create or discover work that exhibits your nature and values, or you will forever toil with the masses that don't. As you look around you can find examples of people who successfully discovered and enjoyed blissful work. At this point in your reading, you are reminded to think of your own brilliant examples of people you admire professionally. Then allow their paths to teach you their salient principles. It was Leonardo da Vinci who taught us: *Those who can copy—can do.*

You may be in awe of others who from the time of their youth seemed destined for their work. These fortunate few seemingly picked their perfect vehicle of work at an early age. They confidently assumed their posts without obstruction. How did they find and follow their unique work? Did they read or somehow visualize their own employment classified advertisement?

Appreciation is a wonderful thing: It makes what is excellent in others belong to us as well.

Voltaire
French writer

The American singer/songwriter Bob Dylan is another bicyclist I hold in high regard. Bob Dylan's music exhibits his essence, nature, and *will*, just as assuredly as Frank Lloyd Wright's architecture and Pablo Picasso's art. The world is filled with thousands of successful cyclists working along all lines of professional endeavor. Any ordinary business is exalted when it is tackled with the spirit of a master instead of its slave. For example, the happy and contented bricklayer has obtained professional self-actualization as uncompromising and fixed as any famous artist. This is certainly true if his work deposits treasure into the accounts of his mind, body, and soul. There is always room for a thoroughbred in any occupation.

> *I like living, breathing better than working...my art is that of living each second, each breath is a work which is inscribed nowhere, which is neither visual nor cerebral, it's a sort of constant euphoria.*

Marcel Duchamp
French-American painter and sculptor

My childhood sports hero Jerry West—voted one of the top fifty basketball players of all time—found his work at a young age. Who among your heroes similarly found his professional calling and stayed with it? Who is it that spurs your fascination? These defining bicyclists will tell you something about yourself if you pay attention. Your heroes, much like the Four Fountainheads that reveal and drive your desire, will and love, are another piston-stroke of the engine, propelling you toward something important. As you become more aware than ever before, it is imperative to write your thoughts down in your journal. This way your thoughts become tangible, more usable assets on which you can always rely.

What attracts my attention shall have it.

Ralph Waldo Emerson
American writer

Thinking about people you admire is like viewing an image of your best self through a translucent window, to be imaginatively pushed open if you so choose. Be bold when approaching this choice. After all, why tiptoe through life trying to safely reach the end? Go for it. Find your livelihood; that lofty vehicle of success.

Success often comes to those who dare and act; it seldom goes to the timid who are ever afraid of the consequences.

Jawaharlal Nehru
Prime Minister of India

Robert Zimmerman Goes Job Hunting

A musician must make his music, an artist must paint, a poet must write if he is to ultimately be at peace with himself.

Abraham Maslow
American psychologist

Consider the following story which makes the point that your genuine work emanates from within; flowing from your true values, which reveal a hyper-linked purpose. The discovery of your true work always occurs from within and flows outward. In architecture it is said that form follows function. When discovering your work, it is function that follows form.

Function following form is your recipe for success. But first one point: all the successful cyclists that have been illustrated in these pages are no doubt emblematic of this book's philosophy and message. But the question remains—could these archetypical bicyclists teach this book's message in a logical and cogent manner to you or me?

Frank Lloyd Wright and the others mentioned in this book arguably employed these principles instinctively, on a subconscious level. They may have been incapable of appreciating or even understanding this fact. If asked to explain the use of the principles directing them to their ideal work, they may have had difficulty articulating them. Upon being asked the question, "Why do you do your work?" they may have merely responded by saying, "I simply do what I love." These bicyclists may have found it difficult to successfully teach the processes necessary for finding true work. This is actually a common phenomenon, and there is no reason why this paradox should not apply here.

Those that know, do. Those that understand teach.

Aristotle
Greek philosopher

For example, ever notice how the most gifted athletes are not usually the ones who become exceptional coaches, capable of teaching the X's and O's of the game? Consider NBA coach Phil Jackson, who coached his basketball teams to eleven NBA championships. This superb coach spent most of his playing days sitting alongside Coach Red Holzman with the

New York Knicks. Phil Jackson was not the most gifted athlete. But he eventually became a highly effective teacher and a Hall of Fame coach.

The last one now, will later be fast, the times they are a-changin'

Bob Dylan
American singer & songwriter

On the other hand, Michael Jordan—recognized by many as the greatest player of all time—never did become one of the great coaches of the sport. In fact, he never became a coach. This illustrates a key point. Each of us needs a structured, step-by-step process for navigating the career-defining steps that these brilliant bicyclists performed quite naturally. It is worth appreciating the fact that not everyone is born equally adept in the art of discovering their life's work. The good news is that you don't have to be. You just need to utilize principles that will direct and illuminate the way toward your work.

It is difficult to imagine Bob Dylan ever looking through a classified section for his employment. Just imagine him sifting through classifieds while wondering what job would bring out the best in him—which job would stoke his passions and allow him to exercise his talents.

The Story

Robert Zimmerman, a seventeen–year-old growing up on the Iron Range of northern Minnesota, contemplates what work would apply his gifts and exercise his nature. Prospects for such employment appear dim

in his hometown of Hibbing, Minnesota, so he decides to hitch a ride to
New York City. Upon arriving, full of anticipation and hope, he peruses
the employment classifieds in the *New York Times*. He soon sees an ad
that speaks to something deep within his soul.

Wanted

Creative musician capable of changing the cultural landscape
of a generation while becoming a national icon. Must have the
talent to write songs with such wide and enduring appeal that
they will be performed and recorded by many other musicians.
Desire to sing is more important than ability and talent. Adhering to the rules and structure of music not nearly as important
as having 'something to say' through original/outside-the-box
renditions. Ability to play the guitar, a must. Talent playing the
piano and harmonica is a plus. Must have determination and
staying power while remaining true to self. A willingness to ex-
periment musically and change name to Robert Dylan required.

Bob Dylan, the poet and musical icon who fatefully walked out the
front door of his home in Hibbing, Minnesota as a seventeen-year-old,
arguably changed the cultural DNA of a generation. Of course, he never
actually saw this classified ad. However, interestingly enough, he got the
job anyway. He filled the position and continues to perform the work in
rather stellar fashion. Dylan's groundbreaking songs came from his open
heart and mind, and surely not an open music instruction booklet. Is
this a foolish example of someone finding their superb bicycle? Actually,
it is anything but. Your desire to find your best is not foolhardy at all. It
is your life's calling.

There is a time in every man's education where he arrives at the conviction that envy is ignorance, that imitation is suicide, that he must take himself for better, for worse, as his portion.... I suppose no man can violate his nature... Insist on yourself, never imitate. That which each can do best, none but his Maker can teach him... Where is the master that could have taught Shakespeare? Shakespeare, will never be made by the study of Shakespeare.

Ralph Waldo Emerson
American writer - Essay on Self-Reliance

If I am not I, who will be?

Henry David Thoreau

So here you are wondering how these bicyclists find such wonderful jobs. How are these bicycles claimed by their owners? Arriving at your unique answer likely requires a paradigm shift.

If you hear a voice within you say, 'You cannot paint', then by all means paint....And that voice will be silenced.

Vincent Van Gogh
Dutch painter

Picturing our archetypal bicyclists looking through the employment classified section of a newspaper, pursuing the Internet for jobs, or participating in a career workshop is hard to imagine. Yet these bicyclists found and rode their defining bicycles throughout their lengthy lives.

Professional happiness is the tonic of longevity. They pedaled and cycled at their chosen task, as their work brought out their personal best in a profession deeply important and wonderfully rewarding.

Do the things you know, and you shall learn the truth you need to know.

Louisa May Alcott
American author

How can you experience an evolution of discovery—part science, part art—that is capable of transporting you to your distinct career and special work? Is there a systematic avenue that mere mortals can travel, bringing us to the same professional conclusion? Take solace; you are about to find out.

Love is a better teacher than duty.

Albert Einstein
German-born physicist

Find, follow, and appreciate the reason *why* you wish to discover your splendid bicycle. A deeper understanding of the genesis of your desire to find your authenticity will not lead you awry. We all need our *why's*. Your reasons—your *why's*—are important. The reason for wanting to find work that exhibits your best existed long before you began reading this book. Hopefully, these early chapters have galvanized and shed light on the factors that will drive you to discover and perform the work for which you are elegantly engineered.

The two most important days in your life are the day you are born, and the day you find out why.

Mark Twain
American author

He who has a why, can endure any how.

Friedrich Nietzsche
German philosopher

Indeed, why find your bicycle? Remember that mirrored question asked earlier—why not? Simply asking, "Why not?" seems to clear the air. In addition, it amplifies an even better question at this point in your reading. And the question is, "it's not who's going to allow you to find your destiny, but who's going to stop you?"

It is the first of all problems for a man or woman to find out what kind of work he or she is to do in this universe.

Thomas Carlyle
Scottish philosopher

Part III

How to Find your Bicycle

The real voyage of discovery consists not in seeking new landscapes, but in having new eyes.

Marcel Proust
French author

Few have been taught to any purpose who have not been their own teachers.

Joshua Reynolds
English artist

Chapter 14

Introduction

Each man has his own vocation. The talent is the call.
There is one direction in which all space is open to him.
He has faculties silently inviting him thither to endless
exertion. He is like a ship in a river: he runs against
obstructions on every side but one; on that side all
obstruction is taken away, and he sweeps serenely over a
deepening channel into an infinite sea.

Emerson
American writer - *Essay on Spiritual Laws*

Where your talents and the needs of the world cross, there
lies your vocation.

Aristotle
Greek philosopher: 384 B.C.-322 B.C.

There is an essence in every person, and in that essence lives the desire
to exist according to one's nature. To live according to this nature, one
has to work from it. But how is this accomplished? Is it really possible
to work and live from the essence of one's nature, or is this just the
idealistic thought of a dreamer? Answers to questions like this don't have

to be complicated to be true. In the same manner the bicycle is not a complicated machine. It is brilliant, but it's not complicated.

Part III of this book will explore principles, assert exercises, and reveal questions designed to help you feel and bring to the surface the foundational building blocks of your nature. Visualize in your mind's eye performing your consummate work while realizing your maximum potential. Imagine reaping the greatest professional enjoyment possible. Being in tune to one's *will* and working accordingly shears the malaise of *inauthenticity*. This in turn helps create the foundation of an inspired life.

And so rock bottom became the solid foundation on which I built my life.

J. K. Rowling
British novelist

Having a better understanding of the reasons why you seek your authentic work now centers the pressing question whose answer eludes all who don't ask, and so many of the heroic that do: how does one actually define and discover one's work? Is there a systematic and pragmatic approach to enlighten the way? Furthermore, can this approach be duplicated by any seeker who desires rewarding and sincere work?

No matter what it is you have previously done, you are capable of finding and traveling a pathway to authenticity. Every truthful purpose has a conduit of discovery; a universal demand for blissful work creates the supply.

There is always a supply to meet any demand.

Florence Scovel Shinn
American artist

You are spurred to seek your ideal work because your head knows and your heart feels as though it certainly exists. Living a genuine and proper professional life is a magnificent ideal of the highest order. Your work, probably more than any other activity, enhances or debases the rest of your life. This ultimately dictates the quality of your existence.

We neither strive for, nor will, neither want, nor desire anything because we judge it to be good: on the contrary we judge something to be good because we strive for it, will it, want it, and desire it.

Baruch Spinoza
Dutch philosopher - Scholium

The question to be explored in this chapter is *how?* How do you find your blissful work? We begin with a thought from the philosopher Baruch Spinoza, who said to ultimately know something one has to know the cause behind it. Spinoza's exact words were, "The knowledge of an effect depends on, and involves, the knowledge of its cause."

Therefore, to understand *the thing*, one must persevere to understand the cause of *the thing*. The following insights and activities will focus your energy and intellect on life's paramount task—to explore the *cause* and mechanics of finding and following your work. The metaphoric bicycle will brilliantly clothe the formula. The bicycle makes the metaphysical act of discovering one's authentic work physical, and thus understandable. As you proceed through these exercises, it will be important to maintain a positive and expectant attitude. This is what William James called *precursive faith*.

How can I be useful, of what service can I be? There is something inside me, what can it be?

Vincent van Gogh
Dutch painter

The purpose of Part III is to help you feel and experience the essence of your unique engine.

Those things that nature denied to human sight, she reveals to the eyes of the soul.

Ovid
Roman poet

Identifying and examining what you value will illuminate your path to your work. You are about to explore various avenues and methods—both metaphysical and physical—that will aid you in identifying your values, which are ultimately steeped in your essence.

But first a word of caution: Some of these activities will be effective and meaningful to you, and some won't be. As you proceed, be especially alert for the key questions and exercises that speak most stridently to your *being* and *nature*. You will know the correct sensation as it happens, and you will *have* to know, since no one can feel this for you. Learn to trust Emerson's admonition: *what attracts my attention shall have it.*

Go to your bosom: Knock there, and ask your heart what it doth know.

William Shakespeare
English dramatist

There is no instinct like that of the heart.

Lord Byron
British poet

Chapter 15

Sisyphus's Dilemma

You have learned about the ancient Greek figure Sisyphus, who was doomed with the futile work of pushing a boulder up a mountain. Upon reaching the top, the boulder instantly rolled back down to the bottom. This was his life; fruitless, unrelenting, repetitive, and worse— unimportant labor. Beginning each day, his hourglass, filled with uninspiring work, was simply flipped over and primed for another day.

In *The Myth of Sisyphus*, Albert Camus noted that as Sisyphus walked back down the mountain to retrieve his boulder, he certainly would have had time to contemplate his fate. We can learn from American philosopher Richard Taylor in his essay *The Meaning of Life* what this time of repose revealed.

After just completing another trip up the mountain, Sisyphus watched forlornly as his rock began to tumble back down the mountain-side. Hanging his head, he took a deep breath and began his descent. Sisyphus, like most everyone, wanted to improve the nature of his work and make it more meaningful. He pondered over how his work could be advanced.

He began by imagining that instead of a boulder, he was fated to transport only a small pebble up a hill. Then he wondered if this change would be what he was seeking from his work. He figured that the pebble would still roll back down the hill, but it would just be a pebble. It would be easy to retrieve and then transport back up the hill. So he asked himself: "Would this improve the condition of my work?" After a bit of thought he confessed that this change would help physically, but sadly it would only help this way.

Upon further reflection, Sisyphus had a thought. He envisioned an even bigger improvement: he imagined that the big boulder didn't roll back down the mountain at all. Now these boulders would begin to accumulate in a pile on top of the mountain. A smile came to Sisyphus as he visualized that if this were so, his efforts would at least produce something, if only just a pile of rocks atop his mountain of work. He was pleased with the idea that his work would actually create something—even if it was just a random pile of rocks and pebbles. But his smile was short-lived, for he felt this new development had not sufficiently improved his condition in a meaningful way.

> *Dear reader: The exercises previously referred to begin here. You must draw your own conclusions about Sisyphus's dilemma. Finding your best requires you to do your own thinking. And meaningful thinking means hard-pressing yourself against a psychological grindstone, knowing the sparks will fly more brilliantly the harder you press. Finding your personal best is not a spectator sport.*

Sisyphus suddenly remembered learning in his youth that honest work should be hard in nature and long in duration. So he considered for a moment that the stone he was fated to transport was extra large, or that the slope was steep and long. Visualizing this change, he saw himself staggering to hoist the stone to his shoulders, as opposed to mercifully pushing the stone up the mountain as the gods had allowed. He wondered if his work would be more meaningful if he did it this way. It did not take long for this idea to leave him *cold*.

Suddenly, Sisyphus had an insight—the gods who condemned him to this unrelenting work were, no doubt, busy conducting their many godly duties. He wondered if they could really be vigilant about watching him work. He began to think, "Maybe they're not watching me at all." And if this was the case, he might be able to abandon his boulder and rest for a bit. Yes, he might be able to rest eternally and experience the life of eternal leisure. Mentally playing this notion out, he realized that such inactivity would only cause eternal boredom. He was aware that this would become a curse unto itself. After all, Sisyphus knew he was immortal, and a bored immortality would be as eternally damning as his fated labor. His vigor fell slack at the thought of it, which was very unsettling. Eternal rest and leisure were obviously not the answer to his dilemma either.

Feeling frustrated, Sisyphus turned his thoughts to other ways he could improve his work. As the weeks passed, the pile of rocks grew quite large. One day he stopped and surveyed his rock pile. He reflected for a moment and rearranged a few stones, configuring them to a pattern he had seen before. Realizing he had to transport his rocks up the mountain, for that he couldn't change, he began to grasp the idea that he could construct something. Yes, he thought. He would build some type of structure. However, he knew he *must* use the plans of another designer or architect, because he was just a lowly hill climber, and what did he know? This idea brought the biggest smile to his face yet, as he suddenly felt his fate had dramatically improved. He would intelligently build something, and with the help of another person's imagination, it could even be beautiful. In this scenario, has his work been elevated to a higher state? Yes, no, somewhat, or just slightly? You decide.

As the years passed, Sisyphus found that he yearned for more. He considered that there must be something more to life than working from the vision and plans of someone else. This job was too small for him. He felt that he really couldn't put his spirit into it. He had tried, but it wouldn't fit. He recognized that he had matured during his work based on someone else's plans. He considered that maybe he should craft something that would bring out his very best—something that spoke to him. Even though his hands had calloused from transporting the rocks, he still longed to *feel himself* in his daily work. He contemplated this idea on the only respite he enjoyed; on his repeated trek down his mountain of work to fetch his rocks. Just as Sisyphus descended his mountain, psychologically mount yourself on his broad shoulders, from where you can enjoy complete relaxation as you think about his dilemma, your dilemma—a universal dilemma.

I have hung all systems on the wall like a row of useless hats. They do not fit.

William Golding
British author

Sisyphus contemplated what the next evolution of progress in his work would look like. In a fit of frustration—and perhaps insanity—he tore down his hard-won structure. He cried and asked, "What have I done? I have people who depend on me. I shouldn't be so self-centered. I'm irrational. So what if I feel like I'm fated to create something special? Maybe it's just my fantasies playing tricks on me. Who am I, really?"

Sisyphus wished to escape the unsatisfied longings and stifled ambition eating away at the heart of his desire. There was an unmistakable undercurrent of *inauthenticity* in his work that would not leave him alone. He felt that if he was to live an honest life, he had to find a way to act from a sincere impulse, emanating from somewhere he didn't know. He was attracted to this idea and thought to himself that one day he would listen and act on his inner impulse, but not today. Today he would remain *comfortably numb*, living among all the sane people pushing insane rocks. Among the sincere, living an insincere existence, and among all the critics, smiling hypocritical smiles. After all, it was safe here. A nodding society agreed.

I was part of that strange race of people aptly described as spending their lives doing things they detest to make money they don't want to buy things they don't need to impress people they dislike.

Emile Henry Gauvreay
French anarchist

After many more weeks of contemplating his fate, he came to the conclusion that it was not the things you did in life that could psychologically kill you. It was the things you didn't do. (Maybe even *Immortals* don't really live forever, but rather for an extremely long time. And because of this—they just believe themselves to be immortal. In this manner, they may really be just like the rest of us. Hmmmm…) Sisyphus believed that he deserved to find his destiny as anyone ever created. He yearned to see himself as part of a universal intelligence, never desiring to lead anyone down a wayward path. He concluded that there was really no other choice than to listen, find, and follow.

On an inauspicious day, Sisyphus began the work of creating something from his own imagination, intellect, and impulse. His work suddenly manifested outward what emanated within. Now, every day, he worked as hard as before. And on some days, because of his new found enthusiasm, he worked even harder. His new venture spoke to him with sincerity. He felt more true to himself than he ever had before. By working according to his true nature, Sisyphus began to exhibit and communicates a bit of himself in his daily work. His days were still filled with transporting those darn rocks up the mountain, but now his work created something he deemed valuable. Through his shared essence with humankind, others could also value his work. And because Sisyphus was condemned to this work for eternity, he began to enjoy the thought of immortally. His youth and vitality never seemed to waver or diminish as he worked with great purpose.

Young is an age, but youth is a quality and if you have it you never lose it.

Frank Lloyd Wright
American architect

May your hands always be busy, May your feet always be swift,
May you have a strong foundation when the winds of changes shift,
May your heart always be joyful, May your song always be sung,
And may you stay forever young...

Bob Dylan
American songwriter - Forever Young

Sisyphus's work speaks to him and communicates—not by words but actions—his essence to the world. On the way back down the mountain to fetch another rock, he smiles and suddenly begins to cry. His tears feel warm as they stream through the dust of his face.

The man may teach by doing, and not otherwise. If he can communicate himself, he can teach, but not by words.

Emerson
American writer - Essay on Spiritual Laws

Only creativity is spontaneously rich. It is not from 'productivity' that a full life is to be expected.

Raoul Vaneigem
Belgian writer and philosopher

The French philosopher, Albert Camus concludes in *The Myth of Sisyphus*, that for Sisyphus, "The struggle itself towards the heights is enough to fill a man's heart. One must imagine Sisyphus happy."

Sisyphus closes his eyes and reflects on what authentic work is. He realizes that his soul and its spirit exude an essence that energizes and animates his will. And when this is sensed by his heart, it spurs his desire and appetite for certain outcomes that he can capably bring about. If he did not have the talent to make this real, the thought would never have occurred to him. He realizes that he has become an unobstructed channel between his soul's energized impulse, his mind's faculties, and his natural talents. He knows that he can perform his work which in turn feeds his soul. In this way, a virtuous cycle is completed. He is beautiful and good, for a thing is beautiful if it fulfills its purpose and good if it displays its nature. The essence of a thing is its spirit, and the spirit of a thing is its essence. One does not exist without the other. Now his essence and its nature are displayed in his work. His work speaks to him. Therefore, it can also speak to the world as he creates something of value to others.

In choosing our Life's work, we should choose that which will call the biggest man and woman out of us and not that from which we can coin the most dollars.

Orison Swett Marden
American author - Making Your Life a Masterpiece

Authenticus Manifestus

There exists the infinite Creator,
Creator of Heaven and Earth,
Creator of our Soul

Housed within our Soul
Lies a universal energy,
Conceptualized as our Spirit

This Spirit wishes to display itself
And become known to the world,
Exudes an Essence

This unique Essence lies two steps from our Soul,
And one step from our Spirit.
It both influences and forges our Nature

This Nature, existing in time and
Being three steps from our infinite Soul,
Can be influenced, yet never obliterated by
Environment and other societal forces. It
Instructs and reinforces—what it is we *Will*

This Will, with its attractions and desires,
Directs us, unashamedly, to a place
We can truly Love+

If we simply allow our Will and what it Loves to direct our
Professional and personal activities;
If we can become an unobstructed channel
Between what it is we Will and Love,
And what it is we do, we begin to live our
Spiritually inspired authentic Life.

Chapter 16

Governing Insights

Two master key principles have been described as the big levers to employ in order to get the most out of this book:

- **Become more self-aware**

- **What you think, you become**

These concepts are the two anchoring rails of one track that can transport you to a place of genuineness. In this and the following chapter, five governing insights and two exploring insights will be investigated. In addition, you will come across a number of exercises that will be necessary for you to do. Think of these insights as strengthening the bridge necessary to transport you to your best work. Each insight is another step toward securing your success, while also increasing the efficacy of the exercises. Each of these insights will be briefly outlined so as not to hinder your momentum.

Governing Insight #1: Take Action

I am not a thing—a noun. I seem to be a verb.

Buckminster Fuller
American designer, author, and inventor

In any moment of decision, the best thing you can do is the right thing, the next best thing is the wrong thing, and the worst thing you can do is nothing.

Theodore Roosevelt
U.S. president

Any action is predicated on taking the first step. A long cycling excursion begins with the single stoke of a pedal. Without that first thrust there will never be a second. Taking a first step, no matter how halting and tentative, is the only way to begin. This first step is the equivalent of planting a seed; one that is capable of growing into still more intelligent and purposeful action directed toward discovering your true work. It is better to take a step—no matter how small—than to choose inaction, which only stifles the will's natural impulse. Strange though it seems, once you earnestly begin your journey to authenticity, you are suddenly halfway there.

It is a tremendous act of violence to begin anything. If I am not able to begin, I simply skip what should be the beginning.

Rainer Maria Rilke
Austrian poet

One of the reasons why so few of us ever acts, instead of reacts, is because we are continually stifling our deepest impulses.

Henry Miller
American writer

Governing Insights | 113

To merely read the coming exercises without participating in them squelches your impulse to take action and continues the habit of negation. This may seem innocuous, but it renders future impulses to grow so faint that a Herculean effort will be needed to act on your impulses. Your song—which always wishes to be sung—will grow fainter still. If you feel you cannot take action at this very moment, at least write down any thoughts generated from these exercises into your journal. Thoughts become useful by making noise. In this way, the scratching of a pen on your journal's page—counts. Notes can be reviewed and acted on later. A note gives you hope. The writing of a note is action in itself.

To think is to act.

Ralph Waldo Emerson
American author

Ideas are elusive, slippery things. Best to keep a pad of paper and a pencil at your bedside, so you can stab them during the night before they get away.

Earl Nightingale
American radio personality and writer

You will find the act of participating in these exercises to be liberating. Natural chemicals called endorphins that cause a euphoric sensation will immediately come to your aid. Any sense of procrastination will be abandoned as one forward step paves the way for the next and you suddenly find the Law of Inertia on your side. After all, pedals in motion tend to stay in motion. Action is important. If Pablo Picasso only dreamed of creating his unique works of art and never put paint to canvas, would he have become *Picasso*? If Frank Lloyd Wright's imagination never dripped off the end of his pen, would he have become *Frank Lloyd Wright*?

These bicycling geniuses—alone with their dreams and vision—each did one important thing. Even if they didn't act on their creative impulses right away, they each eventually did take a first step. However small it may have been, they did something with their idea. We must assume many private victories preceded the public ones, as they discovered for themselves that an ounce of doing trumps a pound of contemplation.

> *It is not the sentiments of men which make history, but their action.*

Norman Mailer
American author

Acting on the vision of defining your bicycle may start slow, but this isn't a problem. This is how real work begins. Bob Dylan's earliest shows weren't the famous concert series known as the *Rolling Thunder Review*. His first performances simply featured him, his guitar, and a few cover songs written by his hero, Woody Guthrie. All famous cyclists had idols they admired and emulated. Relish your heroes as you are cut from the same cloth as these true bicyclists. Some of Bob Dylan's first shows were performed in a café in Dinkytown near the University of Minnesota. A handful of people attended as they waited to see the headliner, who's name was not Robert Zimmerman. As you observe people exercising their authentic, defining work with great skill, it is easy to forget that their first efforts often left much to be desired. The common denominator was the choice of taking a first step, no matter how insignificant. As they sat atop their bicycle, they exercised complete control over their paths. As was the case here, you will learn *to do* from the act of doing. If you find yourself saying you are not good at something you truly value, at least add the word *yet* at the end of your declaration.

That which we persist in doing becomes easier to do. Not that the nature of the thing has changed, but our ability, and power to do it has increased.

Ralph Waldo Emerson
American writer

Discovering your work requires creative action on the part of the discoverer. No matter how original your thoughts, they will have to make some noise to have an impact.

Work is Love made visible.

Kahlil Gibran
Lebanese poet

What saves a man is to take a step, then another step. It is always the same step, but you have to take it.

Antoine de Saint-Exupery
French author

Governing Insight #2:

Operate from a Higher Level

Obstacles will look large or small to you according to whether you are large or small.

Orison Swett Marden
American author and publisher

This second insight is a reminder to seek the highest vantage point possible—mentally, emotionally, and spiritually—as you look over the landscape of potential occupations.

The concept of operating at a higher level is explained by Vernon Howard in his book *Psycho-Pictography*:

> *It is like a mountain climber who has scaled certain peaks but wants to go higher. To do this, he must alter his thinking toward himself, not toward the higher peak. He must strengthen his muscles for the longer climb, he must gather additional supplies, he might need special equipment, and so on. If he attempts to climb to a higher peak while using lower-peak equipment he makes defeat and frustration necessary.*

This concept of operating from a higher level is a recurrent theme and is vitally important.

Governing Insight #3:
The Formula of Be—Do—Have

To Be

We are what we think. All that we are arises with our thoughts. With our thoughts we make the world...Be ye lamps unto yourselves; be ye a refuge to yourself. Betake yourselves to no external refuge.

Siddhartha Gautama Buddha
Indian sage

One of the best things to do sometimes is simply to be.

Eric Butterworth
Canadian educator

To be simply means being in touch with your true nature as it is forged by your essence. *To be* describes awareness; striving to live in the present moment. In *The Strangest Secret*, Earl Nightingale clarified how it is that you become what you think about all day long. For example, the medical student pictures herself as a doctor for maybe a decade before actually becoming one. Up until that point, her purpose was being realized only in her *mind's eye*. And this exemplifies an essential step on the way *to becoming*: visualization. Now, and for the purpose of these exercises, it is helpful to be someone who desires to understand the principles of discovering your authentic work.

They can because they think they can.

Virgil
Roman poet

First say to yourself what you would be; and then do what you have to do.

Epictetus
Greek philosopher

Be the change you want to see in the world.

Mahatma Gandhi
Indian leader

To Do

Ultimately, you become by doing. We all learn to do something from the doing itself. How many books on swimming does one have to read before learning to swim? The more you dare to do, the more you can do. Doing something naturally implies taking action.

Most people are focused on the end result of an action—be it success, money, or prestige—conveniently forgetting that they first must *become* and then *do*. Standing in front of the wood stove of life they shout, "Give me some heat—then I will give you some wood," always wishing for some magical end result before taking the necessary first step.

To Have

You know the progression, once you *become* and *do,* then you can *have.* The concept of *having* spawns many definitions. One is to enjoy yourself and your possessions as you live life in your own way. According to Ray Bradbury, the "goal of life and the reason for your life is simply to wake up each morning and love your life."

Discovering your ideal work is fundamental to loving one's life. Bob Dylan is credited with saying, "What is money? A man is a success if he gets up in the morning and goes to bed at night and in between does what he wants."

But what is happiness except the simple harmony between a man and the life he leads.

Albert Camus
French philosopher

The Be—Do—Have formula is found in nature, and this is your cosmic indication that the principle is universally correct. A plant consists of the root, the bud, and the flower: Be—Do—Have.

Thought is the blossom; language the bud, action, the fruit behind it.

Ralph Waldo Emerson
American poet

In the treatment of the things of Nature we very often take the right road. Whereas in the treatment of man we go astray; and yet the forces that act in both proceed from the same source and obey the same law.

Friedrich Froebel
German founder of kindergarten

Governing Insight # 4:

Artist or Scientist?

There are two kinds of truth. The truth that lights the way and the truth that warms the heart. The first is science, the second art. The truth of art keeps science from becoming inhuman; the truth of science keeps art from becoming ridiculous.

Raymond Chandler
American novelist

Do you possess the nature of an artist or the nature of a scientist? Appreciating the difference allows you to grasp why you see the world from a particular frame of reference. Understanding how you naturally view the world channels your efforts and automatically narrows your professional search. Nearly all professions are grounded in either art or science.

The Artist

Seeing the world from the standpoint of an artist means that you feel within before outwardly creating. An artist acts on an inner impulse, creating outwardly according to this impulse. Building upon the nature of an artist, Picasso created over 50,000 pieces of art. Picasso's intrinsic visions and sensations fueled his creative activity. Picasso claimed that he did not paint a subject as it was, but rather as he saw it from within. Given the beauty and at times uniqueness of his work, this is not a difficult thing to believe. Picasso was once told that the lady subject of his painting did not look like his rendition. He simply replied, "She will." The artist's nature—feeling from within and creating without—can be better understood when contrasted against the scientific nature of Albert Einstein.

The Scientist

Einstein was the consummate example of someone who exhibited a scientific nature. His inspiration and work were driven by what he observed. He was motivated into scientific study in order to understand and explain his observations. Albert Einstein's nature demanded that he explore and explain the principles and laws existing behind what it was he was witnessing. He observed phenomena as they occurred outside his mind and body. In turn, his logical nature sought an explanation. This illustrates the essence of a person possessing a scientific nature.

What do your interests and observations reveal about you? Are you an artist or a scientist at heart? Absorbing this self-knowledge allows you to focus your career-defining activities in a way that is supported by your fundamental nature.

Art is more godlike than science. Science discovers; art creates.

John Opie
English artist

Governing Insight #5:

Your Weakness is your Strength

The idea of considering a weakness as a *strength* is obviously counterintuitive. To appreciate how this phenomenon is true, let's first look at how one's *strength* can be a weakness.

A fundamental strategy of the martial art Jiu-jitsu is to use an opponent's strength against him. Here is an example: if the opponent is recognized as having great speed, a fighter may execute moves in an attempt to throw the opposing fighter in the same direction that the opponent's momentum is already taking him. Essentially, the opponent's strength—in this case, speed—is used against him. The opponent's strength is instantly transformed into a weakness to be exploited. Another example: once a heavy opponent has been taken down, the opponent's size and weight become an instant liability. In these examples *one's strength* becomes a *weakness*.

The less effort, the faster and more powerful you will be.

Bruce Lee
martial artist

Sometimes, the tenets of a law exist diametrically opposite and may be used as such. Therefore, one's weakness can become a strength. This is the point of Governing Insight # Five. An apparent weakness can become a natural strength once you find your authentic career path. For example, a highly empathetic man or woman may make a poor businessperson when constantly faced with bottom-line decisions, such as having to terminate employees. This can be true even when employees warrant being fired. The appropriate act of termination may not be the strength of an overly empathetic leader.

However, in another professional environment this sense of empathy can become a person's strength of the highest order, and even a prerequisite for success. A case in point is that of a highly effective schoolteacher. Teachers mentor, lead, and coach students who are in need of empathetic and positive feedback. A struggling student will almost always appreciate a leader with empathy. Suddenly, what may be a weakness in another situation becomes a critical strength. In this case, a change of professional scenery is responsible for the transformation. A cyclist's weakness becomes the same cyclist's strength when exercising an authentic bicycle.

No man can be ideally successful until he has found his place. Like a locomotive he is strong on the track, but weak anywhere else.

Orison Swett Marden

American author and publisher

Chapter 17

Exploring Insights

Feeling Trumps Seeing—Picasso had it Right

And now here is my secret, a very simple secret; it is only with the heart that one can see rightly. What is essential is invisible to the eye.

Antoine de Saint-Exupery
French author

Picasso was right when he made the observation: *Life is like a train, and above all, you never get to see the engine.* Mechanical engines are visible, but the engine that *wills* your professional life is not. Therefore, the coming exercises are designed to circumnavigate the realm of sight, allowing your feelings to take center stage. If your prior efforts to gain a glimpse of your engine—which indicate a professional *true north*—have remained frustrated, take heart. Your prior work has not been in vain, for adversity introduces a person to himself.

To know oneself, one should assert oneself.

Albert Camus
French philosopher

Any practical mechanic will tell you that in order to intelligently work on the bowels of an engine, a strong light is necessary. And just like a mechanic you must direct this searchlight within, where it will do the most good. The engine that drives our lives—like any mechanical engine—has many moving parts. But it is your will-inspired values that are the all-important pistons.

Your values automatically direct your focus, which is defined as an intense concentration toward a definite purpose. A well-defined purpose fuels your desire. Desire, which is held with faith and passion, eventually changes into commitment, which in turn produces a virtuous cycle of action. This action fuels, modifies, and instructs, creating even more intelligent action. Action is where the rubber wheels of your bicycle meet the road, as the execution and realization of your vision comes into view.

You can't travel within and stand still without.

James Allen
English philosopher

The governing insights outlined in the previous chapter are designed to establish the proper mindset for discovering your authentic work. These exploring insights will illuminate the course to be traveled.

Exploring Insight #1:

The Three Dimensions of Time

Time's trinity of past, present, and future make up our three lifetimes: one lived, one living, and one to be lived. Each of these dimensions holds the promise and power to illuminate the aspiration of finding fit and proper work. By exploring each, a mosaic can be fashioned that leads to a more complete picture of your proper work.

The Past

A child can teach an adult three things: to be happy for no reason, to always be busy with something, and to know how to demand with all his might that which he desires.

Paulo Coelho
Brazilian novelist

An example of one way to explore your past is to ask yourself questions like, "What was I doing in a previous job or project where I felt *a moment of complete happiness?*" or, "Can I remember a time when I literally poured myself into a project I was given to complete?" At the time you may have felt as though your work spoke to you. You felt yourself in the work and it brought out your best. And this was the case even if the work was *hard.* Success leaves footprints. Recognize what direction yours were heading when you reflect on these wonderful moments.

Another way to put the past to work for you is to consider an opportunity you regretfully passed-up. With 20/20 hindsight, you may now realize that if you had only tried, you would have pulled it off. Review your missed opportunities with fresh and more experienced eyes to see what can be learned. Is there a theme involved with these moments in time?

The Present

The future is purchased by the present.

Samuel Johnson
English author

Examining your present involves exploring daydreams and subjects you find your mind naturally drifting toward.

You have your identity when you find out, not what you can keep you mind on, but what you can't keep your mind off.

A. R. Ammons
American poet

What is occupying your mind when you turn away from this page for a brief moment? Your daydreams have a purpose. They can clarify and direct you to find and follow what you love. It is a lot of fun to knock down the walls, tear off the covers, and dig up your answers. Your dreams of day and night—always with an audience of one—are doing all they possibly can to help you. It is good to take them up on their suggestions.

I have realized that the past and the future are all illusions. That they exist only in the present, which is what there is and all that there is.

Alan Watts
English philosopher

The Future

Examining the future means mentally placing yourself in novel situations in order to discover what appeals and speaks to you. Project yourself in your mind's eye into new work environments. For example, read about a person or subject you may have never considered reading about before. If you have always read non-fiction works, begin to read some of the classic fiction that has always attracted your attention. Make new friends and casually observe what these friends think, how they think, and what they do for work. Go to a company that is attractive and ask, "Can I work here for whatever you want to pay me?" Do this knowing you only wish to see what it would be like to work in that company, or that particular industry. This way you do so without the pressure of thinking you're making a life-long commitment.

Before we set our hearts too much upon anything, let us examine how happy they are, who already possess it.

Francois de La Rochefoucauld
French writer

Another suggestion is to get online and research different ideas. As you bounce around and drill down from one topic to another, notice the tact and vector of your search. What does it indicate? Visit Internet sites that list quotes and make note of the professions of the authors. What authors grip you, and why do their thoughts resonate with you?

A learned mind is the end product of browsing.

James Michener
American writer

This process of examining the three dimensions of time is like walking down a long dark corridor lined with windows covered by drawn shades. As you step farther down the corridor and open the shades one by one, the corridor grows brighter. Soon you will be standing in a brilliant room, ever closer to discovering your goal.

I like the dreams of the future better than the history of the past.

Patrick Henry
American statesman

Exploring Insight #2:

This or That?

This simple exercise is designed with the understanding that posing a question in the context of "Do I want this or do I want that?" sets up a framework to quickly clarify priorities. Here are some examples of how this idea would work.

Ask the question, "What makes me feel most like myself?":

☐ Exercising or not exercising?

☐ Eating healthy or not eating healthy?

☐ Being my own boss or working for someone else?

- Exercising my sense of style and judgment, or executing the vision of my manager or boss?

- Being myself versus trying to be someone I'm not?

- I would be more excited if my work's purpose was _____ versus what I am currently doing.

> *I need only consult myself with regard to what I wish to do; what I feel to be right is right, what I feel to be wrong is wrong; conscience is the best casuist: and it is only when we haggle with conscience that we have recourse in the subtleties of argument.*

Jean-Jacques Rousseau
Genevan philosopher

These Exploring Insights, just like the Governing Insights before, are more tools to place in your toolbox. They are points of support to secure your success; additional trusses, under an ever-strengthening bridge.

As you read and work through the coming exercises, keep in mind (and this is very important) to only spend time on exercises that make sense for you. That is, focus on the ones that really *move the needle*. Take the time to discern if the activity's result really speaks to you. If a particular exercise does not help once you try it, feel free to skip it and move on. However, if a particular exercise is difficult but helps, you must continue to work with it. Not all questions, activities, and exercises presented here are to be used by every reader wishing to discover their work. However, woven into this book is a personal philosophical thread for you to grasp and weave into your own cloth of legitimacy. Therefore, listen, feel, and then work with the exercises that you find most beneficial. Most importantly, take a step today, even if it's only a small one.

As if you could kill time without injuring eternity.

Henry David Thoreau
American author

Chapter 18

Enlightening Questions Arouse
Illuminating Answers

It is not the answer that enlightens, but the question.

Eugene Ionesco
Romanian playwright

What you are is a question only you can answer.

Lois McMaster Bujold
American author

Asking a question naturally implies a desire to learn something. Without this desire there would be no need for the question. The question becomes a tool of your desire and can be thought of as an illuminating container holding the promise of something valuable. And the question's mark, once inverted, becomes the fishhook poised to catch your answer. If necessary, bait the hook with your own flesh, for alas, a nibble! This promising nibble leads to another, which can ultimately be your answer. Having the desire to ask a question means that you are gifted with the power to answer it.

Your life, and the work you pursue, represents answers to questions both you, and others, have asked of you since birth. This makes the design and nature of your questions vitally important. Until now, the structure and focus of the questions you have posed to yourself may have been anything from haphazardly beneficial to downright detrimental or destructive.

A prudent question is one-half of wisdom.

Frances Bacon
English philosopher

You are about to explore a wide range of purposeful, enlightening questions. As you read through the questions, become aware of the relatively few captivating questions that speak to you. Pay special attention to the questions that transfix you; there is a reason for your allure. Don't worry about the size of the list. There will be precious few questions that cause you to feel the rhythm of your willful engine. Make this easy on yourself. Do these exercises as you should think and work; that is, according to your nature. An eagle wishing to cross the lake never considers or employs the hard work of a swim.

The soul never thinks without a picture.

Aristotle
Greek philosopher

We have only these questions for which we are in a position to find answers.

Friedrich Nietzsche

German philosopher

Identifying a few questions of consequence that speak to something within can take place abruptly and indiscriminately. Formulating a meaningful answer may take time, but don't be surprised if you grasp an insight or intuition. Intuition, as noted earlier, was the third and highest form of knowledge for the philosopher Spinoza. Answering insightful questions often requires reflection and thought, but don't discount your instincts just because they appear easily. Your success will not be the result of how strenuously you labor; just feel and listen.

Why need you choose so painfully your place, and occupation, and associates... For you there is a reality, a fit place and congenial duties.

Ralph Waldo Emerson

American writer - Spiritual Laws

On the other hand, patience may be needed as you await your answers. And here again, nature is our model. Nature only produces results when they are ready. For example, a mother hen must roost on her newly hatched egg for a full 21 days before her chick appears. No matter how anxiously the committed mother hen parks herself on the egg, or how many mother hens an impatient farmer rounds up to sit on this egg, a law of nature declares that it will be 21 days before the egg hatches: a law as absolute as the law of gravity.

The Quality of Your Questions Dictates the Quality of Your Answers

You can tell whether a man is clever by his answers. You can tell whether a man is wise by his questions.

Naguib Mahfouz

Egyptian novelist

Before you get to the questions themselves—and in an effort to demonstrate the premise and value of asking precise questions—let's explore one universal human desire. You want your life and work to bring you to a state broadly understood as *happiness*. When people are asked the question, "What do you want from life?" most will reply, "To be happy." Broad questions and predictable answers are uttered in every corner of our lives. Unfortunately, asking these meaningless questions will get you nowhere. And the reason—in the example used above—is because the question is too broad, and therefore flawed. This results in a flawed answer that only leads to frustration. But changing a slight nuance of the question immediately makes it more revealing.

For example, a better question than, "What do I want to do for work?", would be to ask, "What would be exciting to do for work?" In attempting to answer this question, a critical lesson is learned. This slight change unveils a distinction that leads you to a more meaningful answer. Asking correct and insightful questions will lead you to illuminating answers that have the power to actually take you somewhere—to your splendid work. By asking purposeful questions, more exact and meaningful answers are sure to follow.

The upcoming questions are designed to work this magic. Each question holds the power to bring to the surface your true essence, which fuels your *will* and reveals your values. Be patient as you consider each question. Continue to write in your journal and make note of the questions that speak to you, along with your instructive answers. As you continue to keep your journal, review your most important questions and answers. According to philosopher James Allen, "You are today where your thoughts have brought you; you will be tomorrow where your thoughts take you."

Once the question has entered your conscious mind, its servant—your subconscious mind—may need time to manifest your unimpeachable answer. Your subconscious committee, ever working for or against you, will now be warmly holding hands and working for your benefit. Upon writing down and sharpening your thoughts, look for common themes. Remember, these answers are yours alone, so it is important that you listen to yourself. There is no one else who can do your listening.

Consider this story that will offer some insight:

Imagine yourself surrounded by a crowd of people. A dozen voices shout at once, telling you what you want. They insist that you want fame, fortune, power, and so on. You spin around, believing each voice in turn. No wonder your (sic) bewildered. But you get tired of all the shouting, so you slowly walk away. The voices become fainter and fainter. Finally, and for the first time in your life, you hear yourself. And now— great day—the inner voice tells you what you really want from life. Now, let me ask you a question: Now that you can hear your inner voice, what does it tell you that you want?

Vernon Howard
American author

As you peruse these questions, strive to listen from a higher plane than you have in the past. The following story illustrates this point:

The citizens of a village in a deep valley were troubled. Floods regularly swept down the valley to carry away their home and livestock. Great boulders from the mountain slopes thudded into their streets and yards. Their children stumbled into the marshes. It was a hard life, but the only one they knew. But one day a Man with Insight, came to town. He told them, "The problem is not the floods and boulders and marshes. The problem is you. You are unnecessary living on a low level." "An unnecessary low level?" they echoed. Yes. Try to understand. Your low level involves you in one crisis after another. As long as you dwell down here, you will have trouble. Raise yourself. Problems will cease to happen." "Show us how!" they pleaded. So the Man with Insight, showed them how to build homes above the valley and on the mountain slopes. Some built new homes a short way above the level of the valley. Others, more wise, built new homes far up the mountainside. "Now", said the Man with Insight, "you will experience the trouble-free life. By moving your residence, you have removed the problems."

*"Yes,"someone remarked, "How clear it now is." "I wonder,"
someone else added, "why we didn't see it before?"*

Vernon Howard
American author - Psycho-Pictography

A wide array of instructive and illuminating questions is listed below. I encourage you to read through the entire list in an effort to gain an overview of their nature. You will find the questions arranged in the categories: Past, Present, and Future. Take your time as you explore them. As you work through this exercise, it is important to know that not only will your answers arrive but, more importantly, so will your questions. You only need to focus and concern yourself with the relatively few questions that truly resonate within you. A rouse of sincerity materializes as you discover *your* questions. Build your journal around these powerful questions.

It is not every question that deserves an answer.

Publilius Syrus
Roman writer

As you ask, answer, and reflect on *your questions*, look for themes and ideas that stand out for you.

*Always the beautiful answer, who asks a more beautiful
question.*

E.E. Cummings
American poet

The only interesting answers are those that destroy the questions.

Susan Sontag
American author

Enlightening Questions

Framed in the Past:

If we would have new knowledge, we must get a whole world of new questions.

Susanne Langer
American philosopher

- [ ] What was I doing in a previous job when I was in a moment of full-bodied happiness? Why?

- [ ] What project was I working on when I found myself totally committed to its completion, and why?

- [ ] What is the most exciting thing I have ever done in my life? Why?

- [ ] Recall a time in your life when you felt you were totally on the right track. What were you doing?

- [ ] Which of my talents brings me the greatest joy?

I'd asked around 10 or 15 people for suggestions. Finally, one lady friend asked the right question, 'Well, what do you love most?'

Andy Warhol
American artist

☐ Recall an instance when you were working and lost all track of time. What were you doing?

☐ Comprise a list of your inspirations and intuitions, including subjects and ideas you find yourself constantly thinking about, but have not acted on? Rank them, starting with the one you think about the most.

☐ Have you ever had a moment of intuition that won't leave you alone?

☐ In a moment of inspiration, what were you told to do? Can you bear to listen? Do you have the courage to act?

☐ Recall a time that you found yourself very creative, and consider what brought out your creativity?

☐ Once, when I _____, it was *like a duck taking to water.*

☐ Once, when I learned _____, it was like lightning striking.

☐ _____ has always been my delight.

- Have you ever come across a thought, idea, or a book when you instantly felt like you had found a goldmine? What was the essential nature of this revelation? Where could it lead you?

- While doing _____, I caught myself smiling and no one was around.

- What did you want to do for the world when you were a child?

Man is most nearly himself when he achieves the seriousness of a child at play.

Heraclitus
Greek philosopher

- What one or two childhood images caused your heart to open up?

My whole life is waiting for the questions to which I have prepared answers.

Tom Stoppard
English dramatist

Enlightening Questions

Framed in the Present:

Trust that little voice in your head that says, "Wouldn't it be interesting if _____," then do it.

Duane Michals
American photographer

☐ If work was a game, what game would you play? Why?

Play is the highest expression of human development...for it alone is the free expression of what is in a child's soul.

Friedrich Froebel
German founder of kindergarten

We don't stop playing because we grow old; we grow old because we stop playing.

George Bernard Shaw
Irish dramatist

☐ If you were a champion of something what would it be? Why?

☐ Imagine that a great disaster befalls you and all may be lost unless you take some type of action. What action would it be? What is your role?

| The ethical reason for business is service to others, so what moves you the most? Whom do you most want to serve?

I slept and dreamt that life was beauty; I woke and found that life was duty.

Lord Byron
British poet

| What topic(s) do you enjoy thinking, reading, and learning about the most? Why?

| What subject would you think you naturally know best?

The thing we know best are the things we haven't been taught.

Luc de Clapiers
French poet

What we know best, only our creator could teach us.

Ralph Waldo Emerson
American writer

| People are constantly thanking me for doing _____.

| My light would shine brightest if my work was _____?

☐ You view a list of famous people having this simple format:

	Name	**Profession**
Example:	Hemingway	Writer
	B. Franklin	Printer
	Your Name	_____

☐ If you could start *fresh* with a clean slate, what direction would your professional life take? (Don't worry about actually having the clean slate, just imagine what you would do.)

☐ If shooting at the target of your life, what is the picture in the bulls-eye?

☐ An imaginary and rather forward stranger asked, 'Tell me about you'. Your ideal answer is _____.

☐ What historic figures do you admire most? Why?

☐ Simply ask, "What am I really trying to do?"

☐ My work is a creative problem to be resolved, so my first step is to _____.

☐ What one or two people would you like to be mentored by?

☐ What would please the *truth* within?

☐ For what question would the answer be an exclamation point?

If we are honest, then we reveal ourselves, but we do not have to make an effort to be individualistic.

Josef Albers
German artist

- ☐ What is the purpose of my life?

- ☐ My top three talents are: _____, _____ & _____.

- ☐ I work at _____ because it justifies my life.

- ☐ If you were to wake up one morning, for the first time as (your name), who would you be and what would you do?

If we are ever in doubt about what to do, it is a good rule to ask ourselves what we still wish on the morrow that we had done.

John Lubbock
British banker and scientist

- ☐ What are you so confident of that you would promote and defend in an egotistical manner for the first time ever?

- ☐ _____: This is what I want to be.

- ☐ What would you be so sure of that you could only do in your own way?

☐ What do you see as the most critically unmet need that you could positively impact?

☐ What do you most want to do something about?

☐ It is tragic when one is never bitten in life by true inspiration. What has been your deepest *bite* so far?

☐ If I was simply honest with myself, I would _____.

☐ I'm a _____ so that's what I do.

☐ By doing _____, I am following my own personal calling.

☐ I _____, because I need to.

☐ I _____, because I just can't help it.

☐ I'm a _____, because it is the thing I do best.

☐ When I believe it is time to play, I _____.

☐ I _____, because I love it.

☐ I _____, because it is my duty.

☐ I _____ because I want to be remembered for it.

☐ I _____, because, I can't imagine not _____.

☐ If I just follow my intuition, I would _____.

☐ I'm either going to be a _____ or a bum.

☐ When I _____, I am *home*.

☐ You see a picture of yourself with a caption under it. What does it say?

☐ What problem am I uniquely qualified to solve?

☐ What work would create in you a feeling of over-powering enthusiasm?

☐ If you were told by a doctor that you have eighteen months to live, and you must leave something for the world to remember you by, what would you create?

☐ Imagine walking into a pentagon-shaped room. Conjugating within each of the 'corners' are the following collections of people: Scientists, Physicians, Artists, Engineers, and in the last corner a group of Entrepreneurs. Which set would you gravitate to, and what questions, comments, and observations would you bring to the conversation?

☐ You are hosting a dinner party for 6 to 10 people (currently living or not). Who would you invite as your guests? Why?

Tell me, what is it you plan to do with your one wild and precious life?

Mary Oliver
American poet

If you know that your life was merely a phase or short, short segment of your entire existence, how would you live?

Chuck Palahniuk
American writer

Enlightening Questions

Framed in the Future:

- What would you do if you could not fail?

- What would you do if you were ten times smarter than everyone else? What would you do with that intellectual edge?

- What would you do if you were suddenly given 10 million dollars? Now your work or play needs absolutely no relationship to your income.

- What do I want my life to look and feel like?

- What is it just inevitable that I become?

No question is so difficult to answer as that to which the answer is obvious.

George Bernard Shaw
Irish dramatist

What endeavor is actually trying to find me?

What is the purpose or aim of my life?

Your life is a story – It reads_____.

What would you be willing to risk it all for? And why?

Question is made up of: *Quest I On*. What is your life's quest?

Which of my talents was I born to use?

If you could become an associate or business partner of someone – past or present – whom would you pick? Why?

_____ is something I want to do?

At the age of 90, you look back on your life with intense gratification, because you worked at _____ and helped _____.

I don't know if it will be a successful life, but I always saw myself as a _____.

☐ Make a list of two or more broad disciplines of work you have always been attracted to and, using your unique perspective, unite them to form your original work. What profession does this hybrid discipline direct you to pursue?

(Personally, I am drawn to the fields of education, philosophy, and psychology. When these interests were blended with answering the riddle of how to go about discovering one's purposeful work, I was inspired to write this book.)

Imagination consists of taking two or more things that do not exist together, blending them together in the mind, and then creating an emergent third thing that never existed at all.

David Brooks
American author - The Social Animal

As this list of questions concludes, you may find deposited within your heart the quintessential question, holding the answer to, "Who's riding my bicycle?" If this is the case, simply ask and answer that question. No one holds a monopoly on listing illuminating questions.

No man really becomes a fool until he stops asking questions.

Charles Steinmetz
German-American mathematician and engineer

Computers are useless; they can only give you answers.

Picasso
Spanish artist

Make a list of everything you love.

Rhonda Byrne
Australian writer

Look at every path closely and deliberately, then, ask ourselves this crucial question: Does this path have a heart? It if does then the path is good, if it doesn't it is of no use.

Carlos Castaneda
Peruvian writer

Chapter 19

What You Value, Clarifies the Way

When your values are clear to you, making decisions becomes easier.

Roy E. Disney
American businessman

The value of a principle is the number of things it will explain; and there is no good theory of disease which does not at once suggest a cure.

Ralph Waldo Emerson
American writer

Your authentic professional path is fueled by your *will* and paved with the bricks of your essence. It rests on a foundation of what you value. The questions in the prior chapter were designed to identify and reveal your interests and appetites, while stoking the fire of your engine. Every exercise you have participated in holds great promise, but this exercise strikes the heart of the matter.

153

*Why not spend some time determining what is right for us,
and then go after that?*

William Ross

American composer

The following exercises are designed to help you identify what you instinctively value. Your values are driven by your nature and fueled by an essence with which you were uniquely endowed. Your first task will be to write down easily identifiable values. Values spur thoughts that cause specific behaviors. This first exercise will ask you to list your obvious and most apparent values. This should not require a lot of thought or take a lot of time.

The Exercise

<u>**Your Values**</u>   <u>**Your Behavior**</u>

I obviously value _____ Because I : _____

I obviously value _____ Because I : _____

To enhance specificity and ensure your Values List is as complete as possible, list at least one value for each of the following categories: family, health, spirituality, mental, money/finances, emotions, areas of interest, lifestyle, work, joy/pleasure, and any other categories important to you. You may have addressed one of these categories and value(s) in the previous exercise. If so, just stay with that answer unless you identify an additional value and a corresponding behavior. In addition, please understand that you may have more than one defining value for a category:

For the category of family: **I value** _____ **so I**

_____

For the category of health: **I value** _____ **so I**

_____

For the category of _____ : **I value** _____ **so I**

_____

...and so on. Write these out in your journal. If you recognize some new, but previously latent values, use the format below. The set-up to express these values is:

Since I have discovered that I value _____, I need to _____

Since I have discovered that I value _____, I need to _____

Value-identifying exercises aid you in successfully answering the question, "Who's riding my bicycle?" As with all these exercises, it goes without saying that it's important to be honest with your self. This exercise—which rests on the supports provided by governing and exploring insights—provides a recipe that is essential for discovering the pistons that will drive your engine toward your work. As an example, here are my values and how they dictate what I do or need to do. Seeing mine may help you complete the exercise for yourself. But the key is to define *your* values.

Happiness is that state of consciousness which proceeds from the achievement of one's values.

Ayn Rand
Russian-born writer

I value	So I
1. A great family life	had to find a fantastic wife and mate
2. Talented caring children	had to be a good father who spawned a stimulating, nurturing environment
3. Creativity	am drawn to artists like Bob Dylan, Frank Lloyd Wright, and others
4. Entrepreneurial success	sought careers with self made people who built their own businesses, such as Tom Monaghan, Rick Schaden, Jim Ferrell, and Kevin Plank of Under Armour, Inc. I also owned and led my own companies.
5. Vibrant health	am physically active and play a lot
6. My independence	don't join social groups easily; working from home takes absolutely no self-discipline because I enjoy it.
7. Intelligence	read non-fiction biographies about accomplished men, and women. I enjoy philosophy, and inspirational quotes.

The wisdom of the wise and the experience of the ages are perpetuated by quotations.

Benjamin Disraeli
British statesman

The simplest schoolboy is now familiar with truths for
which Archimedes would have sacrificed his life.

Ernest Renan

French philosopher

8. Independent thought
I live a non-traditional life, having cultivated my own living philosophy gleaned from observation and experience.

9. Excellence
I buy fewer objects of superior design versus more of cheaper design and value. I appreciate well-crafted cars, furniture, books, systems that work, and athletes who use proper techniques.

10. I value the idea of positively influencing and empowering others in a vitally important area of life—finding of one's true and authentic work. Therefore I *had* to write this book.

The last exercise on this topic is to list what you value above all else. List the one or two values that speak to you most stridently. Focus on the ones that really inspire and move you.

My defining values are _____ & _____.

So, therefore, I need to _____.

Persistence is a great element of success. If you only knock long enough and loud enough at the gate, you are sure to wake somebody up.

Henry Wadsworth Longfellow
American poet

Look within and work at this exercise until your values are well defined. Most importantly, get started today. No one enjoys the luxury of procrastination when it lasts forever.

The timid watch from the sidelines of life while those with confidence battle it out.

Laurence Boldt
American author

In the long run you hit what you aim at, therefore, through you should fail immediately, you have better aim at something high.

Henry David Thoreau
American author

Some additional keys to consider as you work through these exercises:

- Revisit these exercises frequently. Record in your journal your intuitions, and yet exercise patience if necessary. When you are on the right track, you can easily endure a slower, harder, but more interesting journey. Remember the encouragement from Chapter 2: *This game is not over until you win.*

□ Listen, feel, and write in your journal.

□ Review, reflect, and focus

I'm not a very good writer, but I am an excellent rewriter.

James Michener
American writer

Strong lives are motivated by dynamic purposes.

Kenneth Hildebrand
American author

What Don't You Value?

To know one thing, you must know its opposite.

Henry Moore
English sculptor

Identifying what you don't value can be as revealing as understanding what it is you do value. Many discoveries, whether physical or metaphysical, are found by continually taking away what they are not. Gold is found and claimed by the miner who first removes all that isn't gold through the panning process. Once everything besides the gold has been removed, the prized element is exposed.

Therefore, it is helpful to take a minute to ask yourself, "What don't I value?" Is the answer just everything not previously listed as something you do value? No, it likely is not. And the reason is the inherent caveat that we have already learned: broad questions breed broad answers, which are not beneficial to your purpose. You must determine what you don't value with specificity. Knowing what you don't value makes it easier to understand why you exhibit certain traits and habits.

This exercise's format is:

I find myself doing   **Therefore, I must not value**

_____   _____
_____   _____
_____   _____

An example:

I find myself   **Therefore, I must not value**

- Giving money away before I actually have much of it

                                           Money

- Having limited earnings for three years while writing this book.

The Exercise

<u>I find myself doing</u>	<u>So I must not value</u>
_____	_____
_____	_____

This exercise allows you to identify inclinations, tendencies, and habits from the other side of the value equation. Picasso's engine, like most engines, operates in the gears of forward and reverse.

Chapter 20

Defining Your Nature

To become an able and successful man in any profession,
three things are necessary; nature, study and practice.
An artist, under pain of oblivion, must have confidence in
himself, and listen only to his real master: Nature.

Auguste Renoir
French artist

A man never frets about his place in the world, but just
slides into it by the gravitation of his nature, and swings
there as easily as a star.

Edwin Hubbel Chapin
American clergyman

Aristotle said that "where your talents and the needs of the world intersect, there lies your vocation." But what is the genesis of our talents? Could the fountainhead of our talents originate in our spirit's essence, and nature?

If a man has talent and can't use it, he's failed. If he uses only half of it, he has partly failed. If he uses all of it, he has succeeded, and won a satisfaction and triumph few men ever know.

Thomas Wolfe
American novelist

Determining the origins of your innate talents is, granted, an inexact science. Talent could spring from the intersection of one's values and nature. Talent undiscovered and unused leads to frustration and a constant sense of longing or uneasiness. Therefore, it becomes worthwhile to unearth the foundational building blocks of your talents. As noted earlier, to know a thing, one must know the cause of the thing.

Talent is a gift which God has given us secretly, and which we reveal without perceiving it.

Charles de Montesquieu
French philosopher

I stayed away from mathematics not so much because I knew it would be hard as because of the amount of time I knew it would take. Hours spent in a field where I was not a natural.

Carl Sandburg
American poet

Every artist dips his brush into his own soul, and paints his own nature into his pictures.

Henry Ward Beecher
American clergyman

Just as you did in the previous exercises, you will begin this exercise by identifying and listing your most apparent and easily recognizable tendencies. Here is the format for this exercise. No one will see this list but you, so be open with yourself.

In the realm of	**My apparent nature is to**
Emotions	
Intellect/Mental	
Physical	
Play	
Achievement	
Spirituality	
Finances	

Why are we here on Earth? Because we have interior themes to develop and enjoy.

Honore de Balzac
French novelist

Revisit this and all of these exercises from time to time. As you do this, think of your initial answer as something skewered on the spit of a rotisserie. And like any rotisserie cooking over an open fire, it must be turned and explored from every angle possible, over and over again. You will know when it's done.

I have resolved on an enterprise that has no precedent and will have no imitation. I want to set before my fellow human beings a man in every way true to nature; and that man will be myself.

Jean-Jacques Rousseau
Genevan philosopher

The real character of a man is found out by his amusements.

Joshua Reynolds
English artist

Argue with anything else, but don't argue with your own nature.

Phillip Pullman
British writer

To find in ourselves what makes life worth living is risky business, for it means that once we know we must seek it. It also means that without it life will be valueless.

Marsha Sinetar
American writer

Chapter 21

Writing Your Personal Classified
Employment Ad

Make your work your play, and your play your work.

Phil Jackson
NBA coach

Whatever you can do, or dream you can...begin it.
Boldness has genius, power and magic in it.

Goethe
German philosopher

Earlier, we saw a hypothetical employment classified ad that was never written and never seen. Here you will write your own magical employment classified. It will never appear in an employment section of any newspaper. However, as in Bob Dylan's case, you will find that you can eventually fill this wonderful position. How should it read?

You may use the following template, or you may write your own classified ad from scratch.

Wanted

A smart, passionate individual who values _____ and is infused with the purpose to _____. A desire to help _____ and _____ by providing _____(product or service) is necessary. The following traits of _____, _____, and _____ are a must. The candidate will process the following talents: _____, _____, and needs to be proficient in _____ and _____. The ideal candidate will be passionate about _____ and love _____. A strong sense of will power and patience is desirable.

Despite several decades of research, the most effective way to predict vocational choice, is simply to ask the person what he wants.

John Holland
American scientist

Chapter 22

Universal Laws Guide Creative Action

Happy is he who has found the cause of things.

Virgil
Roman poet

The goal of life is to make your heartbeat match the beat of the universe, to match your nature with nature.

Joseph Campbell
American author

Finding and following your work places you at the very center of your life. This is much like the sun is the center of our solar system; a solar system located within a much larger universe. This universe, though vast and complex, is governed by the articles of its constitution. Furthermore, these articles and their laws—forever without amendment—are comprehensible because the universe is a cosmos, meaning there is order in it. To have order naturally means that the universe is governed by laws. And it is a high science of study indeed to work at understanding and operating along the edicts of these incontrovertible laws. These laws apply equally to the physical world of things and the metaphysical world of spirit and thought. If there were no cosmic laws to order our universe, we surely would have descended into a chaos by now. And we have no

169

chaos, as the seasons always arrive in the same order and days are always 24 hours long.

> *A little consideration of what takes place around us every day would show us, that a higher law than that of our will (underline mine) regulates events; that our painful labors are unnecessary, and fruitless; that only in our easy, simple, spontaneous action are we strong.*

Ralph Waldo Emerson
Spiritual Laws

Acknowledging that the universe is governed by laws—and that these are laws we should learn to obey and harness—is not the same as understanding it as fact. True understanding is what you should really seek. However, even gaining understanding and acquiring knowledge is not sufficient, because neither understanding nor knowledge will automatically apply themselves. It is through application that one benefits and truly learns to use these cosmic laws to one's advantage. Knowledge comes most readily to those who have the courage to dare and the faith to do. And moreover, for your courageous work to reach its maximum effectiveness, it must be aligned with the established universal laws that govern our cosmos. If you don't know and understand these laws, you're apt to go against them and get their penalties versus their promises.

Success in discovering and performing your proper work is guided by these natural laws. If we are to obtain and realize the effect we have to first understand and create the cause. Causes spawn effects and all that follows.

Keep in mind that your goal of finding true and value-driven work is a big idea. Large ideas supersede and eventually annihilate smaller ones. This is good news. Holding a large idea with a fixed purpose rids you of the distractions and petty annoyances that are sure to thwart average people who entertain average thoughts; invariably leading to average results.

Three things will bring you to a point where you're pursuing your unique and most rewarding work. Firstly, you must desire it. Secondly, assert your claim for it. And thirdly, take possession of it. Furthermore, you must inject your desire with feeling and exert your will by making a firm demand.

Feeling is the very fountainhead of power. Feeling emanates from within, whereas one's sight can only perceive from without. Feeling gives vitality to your thoughts, while your *will* holds your thoughts steady. Thought is the fire that creates the steam necessary to turn your wheel of fortune. And at this very moment your wheel of fortune is turning, and has always been turning. Having your thoughts and actions aligned with the edicts of established universal laws brings you to a place of lasting success. To find your authenticity, you must align your thoughts and actions with universal law. There are such laws and they cannot be supplanted, at least successfully, for any length of time.

This book encourages you to find and follow your individuality and na-ture, so that you can live among the professionally fulfilled. Your thoughts and feelings create an irresistible combination. Loving the idea of finding your true north imparts vitality to that thought. And it should be very easy to love this idea. The key purpose of this chapter is to point out that your ultimate success in determining who's riding your bicycle—apart from the all-important need to listen to your *will*—depends on adhering to nature's laws. I will highlight a few of these universal laws so you can begin the process of understanding and applying them.

There should be no dispute that natural laws govern the physical world we inhabit. An immutable and easily recognized example is the Law of Gravity. Gravity may be invisible, but it is very real. Gravity's effects are so prevalent and normal that we easily take them for granted. When we witness an apple fall to the ground, we are not seeing gravity per se, but the effect of gravity, or gravity at work. You no doubt learned of the Law of Gravity in school. Some of the other physical laws you probably learned about include: the Law of Inertia, the Law of Equal and Opposite Reaction, and maybe even the Law of Attraction. Something you may not have learned in school is that these physical laws also apply to the metaphysical world of spirit and thought. It will be through understanding and applying these *metaphysical counterparts* that will serve you best in discovering your authenticity. So let's explore a few of these cosmic universal laws.

The Law of Attraction

The Law of Attraction is demonstrated in the physical world when two molecules of hydrogen are attracted to one molecule of oxygen, creating the compound of water. And going back another molecular step, you find that certain atoms have an affinity for others. Once attracted, they form the molecules of hydrogen, oxygen and all the other elements, compounds, and mixtures which make-up the entire earth.

Just as exacting as this and other physical laws that govern the material world are the universal spiritual laws that govern the world of thought,

will, and love. These metaphysical laws act with the same invariable precision and reliability as the laws of physics.

From our earlier discussion, you already know that thoughts are causes
and conditions are effects. The Law of Attraction says that your thoughts
attract certain elements, powers, and people, which in turn cause—or at
least contribute heavily—to your conditions. This leads directly to what
you will eventually achieve and enjoy. When you observe an invention
that was created by Thomas Edison, or Steve Jobs and Steve Wozniak,
you're not seeing the thought that led to the creation. You're seeing the
effects of the thought, or the thought at work. Thomas Edison thought
with intensity about the incandescent light bulb before it appeared before
his eyes. The same principle was exercised by Steve Jobs and Steve Wozniak, when their imaginative thought, coupled with energy and vigor,
caused the first Apple Computer to make its way into our homes. The
thoughts of these renowned inventors always worked. And, in the same
manner, your thoughts always work; whether you are aware of them or
not, and whether their consequences are intended or not.

When it comes to finding authentic work and determining who is
riding your bicycle, it is the metaphysical laws of spirit and thought that
have the upper hand. These universal laws are made tangible when they
are laid bare upon the common bicycle. It is these metaphysical laws that
direct all creative action, and whose true progeny is creative thought. In
this way, the bicycle becomes your laboratory of study for the purposes
of this book. The bicycle symbolizes universal law, thereby making these
invisible metaphysical laws more recognizable, more memorable, and
most importantly, more useful.

To review, the physical universe is governed by natural law.
Furthermore, these laws are not subject to caprice. Therefore, you have

a cosmos (an orderly harmonious systematic universe) and not a chaos (inherent unpredictability in the behavior of a natural system). If the physical universe is governed by physical laws and the thought world is governed by metaphysical laws, the creative act of successfully discovering your most congenial work is also governed by laws, including the Law of Attraction. As is the case with the physical universe, your thought universe is a cosmos rather than a chaos. It operates upon a set of universal thought laws. And these are laws that we can all learn to comply with.

As discussed earlier, successfully discovering your authentic work is predicated on understanding and appreciating your nature and its essence. This is based on knowing what it is you *will*, and what this *will* loves. What your *will* loves is most directly revealed by the aforementioned four fountainheads, out of which flow an essence and nature that will direct your genuine values. In order to understand this concept and the Law of Attraction, we will look to nature itself for direction.

Our nature will attract what belongs to it.

Ralph Waldo Emerson
American author

As humans, we all have the unique ability to think. Therefore, we are a thought-being that operates within a thought world. We are not a body with a mind, but a mind with a body. Similarly, we are not a body with a spirit, but a spirit with a body. And when this body one day dies, it is not the body that surrenders the spirit, but the spirit that surrenders the body. And this spirit, with its one and only ability to think, desires to reveal and communicate itself to an awaiting world.

Your spirit's thoughts can only be revealed through bodily actions, as spurred by your thoughts while you are at work or play. It will be through your thoughts entertained and their actions exhibited that will attract to you the necessary elements of your success. Understanding universal law and putting these laws into practice creates the foundation necessary to discover your vocation. And yet, while these laws are proven and universal, you are the only one who can apply their principles. You are the only one who can do your thinking. Therefore, it is you who controls the attracting. And in the same manner, no one but you can feel the nature and the essence of your spirit. Consequently, you hold the secret of how your spirit wishes to express itself to a curious world. You are endowed with the key to unlock your unique doors, and this is one reason you're encouraged to earnestly take what attracts your attention and use what suits your case; disregarding everything else.

Only a small percentage of people actually work authentically, as directed by their will, nature, and values. All others live in a perpetual state of professional disharmony. By understanding and aligning yourself with the Law of Attraction, you can join the brave and chosen few who work harmoniously to their heart's content. This doesn't mean that you wish to always be at work. After all, bicycling requires balance: A balance between work and play, and everything else you wish to do.

Attraction and the Law of Creative Thought

For you there is a reality, a fit place, and congenial duties. Place yourself in the middle of a stream of power and wisdom which animates all whom it floats.

Ralph Waldo Emerson
Spiritual Laws

Thought is creative and it is a cause; your conditions, work and otherwise, are the effects. Thought originates in your spirit. Therefore, your action is your spirit trying to express itself. Your creative instinct originates in your spiritual nature because spirit can only be creative.

The act of creation is the synthesis of elements that have an affinity for each other in their proper proportion. An earlier example of something being created out of natural attraction is the compound of water, which is chemically denoted as H_2O. Obviously, hydrogen and oxygen have a natural affinity for each other, since water covers 70 percent of our planet. But who is the builder of water and where did these plans originate? You easily understand that a construction foreman cannot build anything until he gets the plans from the architect. However, the architect can only get the plans from his or her imagination. The act of *building, creating, and inventing* is the divine dovetailing with the practical. And this holds true whether we are building a physical structure or building the foundation of a career.

Where then does imagination come from? It emanates from one's spirit, which has at it disposal the boundless energy and intelligence christened the *Universal Mind* or *the Infinite Mind*. To make use of the Universal

Mind, it must be first recognized and then tapped into. And this is the key point to be made at this juncture in your reading.

Creative thinking—the one absolute precursor of anything ever created in the history of this Earth—requires attention. Attention is a powerful weapon because it's through attention that you will develop concentration. This power of concentration and focus is directed by your will, and its power is called *will power*. The most effective way to put your will power to work is not in a futile attempt to will others toward your way of thinking or doing, but to direct your will upon yourself. Keep your will power at home, where it will have the greatest benefit for you and for others.

Therefore, following the edicts of the Law of Attraction, you must refuse to think of or concentrate on anything but that which you really desire. It is through this concentration that your dominant thoughts will attract like-minded people, ideas, materials, knowledge, and all the forces necessary to attain your true purpose.

Your life, actions, and influence in the world will depend on the degree of truth you are able to attract and perceive. And the level of truth you are able to perceive becomes manifested and evident in your character. This is the so-called truth that will set you free. Your awareness and knowledge of truth allows you to overcome every difficulty.

Three key questions: What do you want? What is true?
And what are you going to do about it?

Ray Dalio
Money Manager

As all thoughts are creative by nature—and the truth is the highest and most perfect thought anyone can have—it is clear that to think the truth is to create that which is true. The theory and practice of this depends upon your knowledge of the truth concerning yourself and the world in which you live. One overriding truth to keep in mind is that all of life desires increase of some type. You have your own definition of what *increase* means. This palpable and unwavering desire for increase comes from one's spirit, which seeks fuller expression and a blossoming life.

Our thought, which is creative, comes from our spiritual power, which is the mightiest force of all. Creatively thinking about what work you should do is a cause, and the work you do is an effect. Said another way, finding your most authentic work is an effect, and if you are to obtain the effect you must craft the cause. Therefore, understanding and putting to work the Law of Attraction is paramount for your success.

Whatever we think about can be created in the objective world. Our lives and the work we do are a reflection of our dominant thought-causes and the effects that were sure to follow. Therefore, the future work we do will be dictated by our future thoughts, which will inspire and direct our future actions.

We bring into existence what we think, as likes attract likes. This is the spiritual mirror image of the natural world's law of attraction, which is evident in nature. You are the cumulative reflection of every thought entertained during your lifetime up until this moment. Your prior thoughts are stamped on your face, forged in your form, and revealed in your environment. It's important that you come to grips with this and acknowledge it as fact. Granted, for many this is not easy. The gauges monitoring your two large levers mentioned in Chapter 6—**become more self-aware** and **what you think, you become**—should be *red-lining* at this point.

So how does conscious thought and action—*something you are endowed with complete control over*—play its part in getting you to a state of finding your ideal work and an authentic life? It happens by tapping into and putting to work:

The Subconscious Mind

Thinking is our conscious mind in action, which has as its subject—and under its command—the subconscious mind. The subconscious mind cannot escape from the pictures our conscious mind incessantly projects upon it. Your conscious mind directs the thoughts that go into the subconscious mind, and has been referred to as the watchman at the gate of your subconscious. Furthermore, every thought allowed into the subconscious mind is not unlike a farmer planting a seed in his field. And like the farmer who incessantly plants many seeds of the same type, it can only be that a crop germinating from that exact type of seed will take root and grow. Likewise, your continuity of thought, which has been consciously planted in your subconscious mind, will invariably produce the crop that becomes your life. And like all crops—good or bad—it must eventually be harvested. Therefore, the key questions are:

- What are you thinking?

- What are you creating?

- What is the harvest going to yield?

It has been said repeatedly that the work you perform is an effect, and effects always are associated with causes. To *right* the effect we must create and *right* the cause. Through correct thinking—the wellspring of everything pleasant and correct—we can find and perform work that is authentic and which harmonizes with our spirit, will, and values.

Your subconscious mind is inextricably linked to the *Universal Mind,* with the only difference being one of degree. This idea of being the same as, but varying by degree, is illustrated by a single drop of water taken from the ocean. This one drop contains all the elements of the entire ocean. The only difference is one of degree. Such is the relationship of your subconscious mind to the Universal Mind, or what is sometimes referred to as the Mastermind, the Infinite Mind, or what Emerson called the Over-Soul.

Ultimately, the genesis of it all is your spirit trying to express itself and its essence more fully. Spirit is really all there is of us; because we know that when our spirit has left us, we are nothing. Again, one's spirit possesses the power to think and thus create. Therefore, your ability to think is your link to the Universal Mind. Knowing this, you can make use of it for your purpose, and in turn for the benefit of others. To consciously control thought is to control circumstances, conditions, environment, and in the case of finding your bicycle, your professional destiny. It is the nature of thought to find its way into action.

To conclude, the Law of Attraction is alive in the natural and physical world. Therefore, it is alive and mirrored in the world of spirit and thought. You become and magnetize what it is you think about all day long. Your ultimate success will come from your firmness of vision, your fixity of purpose, and the steadiness of your faith; all while adhering to these universal laws that govern spirit and thought.

The Universal Law of Abundance

Another universal law you will find of value—as you find and follow your work—is the Law of Abundance. Therefore, it behooves you to give it some thought at this point in your reading. It does not take long for the aware person to look around and see that nature is always lavish. Nature is always abundant and lavish, even to the point of being wasteful.

Picture yourself sitting beneath a tree on a bright summer day. You can easily imagine that this would still be a great tree with only a fraction of the normal amount of leaves. But nature, in its lavishness, has chosen to employ ten times that amount. If you pull off one leaf, two may grow in its place. One acorn will produce an oak tree with thousands of acorns, which can potentially produce thousands of oak trees, all capable of producing millions more, and this train of lavish abundance never stops. Yes, nature is generous, and since you are created by the same intelligence and operate under the same laws, it is inevitable that you will reap the same benefits. That is, if you have the desire to recognize, are broad enough to understand, and have the faith and courage to act.

A genius is a man who has an eye to see Nature... a heart to feel Nature... and the courage to follow Nature.

Welsh Proverb

Nature is your guide as we begin to recognize and employ what nature is trying its best to teach. We know that Henry David Thoreau was instructed by the nature surrounding Walden's Pond; the entire world's nature surrounds Walden's Pond. The point is that no matter how large your goals or how much you ask for yourself, this will be a small matter considering the scope of what nature and the universe has available to give. It has been said before— do not approach your ocean of opportunity holding a meager teaspoon wishing it to be filled.

There is enough resources and riches for all, and people are not kept poor because of a lack of supply. The supply is practically inexhaustible and the invisible supply really is inexhaustible.

Wallace D. Wattles
American author

The Law of Equal and Opposite Reaction

The last law to be briefly described is Newton's Third Law of Motion, known as the Law of Equal and Opposite Reaction. When you first learned of this law you were taught that for every action, there is an equal and opposite reaction. Therefore, when your bicycle's wheels grip the road and push the road backward, because of mutual interaction, the road must be pushing the wheels forward with equal force. Consequently, as you push on the pedals of desire to find your most authentic work, the thought universe is obliged to push back and deliver results with equal force and vigor. Certainly everyone desires to engage their precious days in what each would consider their fit and proper work. Yet you don't have to look far to see that the equal and opposite rebound—of fit and proper work—has not been achieved. Therefore, there must be building a tremendous storehouse of this energy awaiting its release, as dictated by this law. It has to be that these thoughts must rebound upon the thinker who understands this, is attuned to their *will*, and is aligned with these aforementioned universal laws. And the good news is that *you* are now one of them!

Certainly there are many more universal laws that could play a part in this discussion. Highlighted here are a few of the most important ones to recognize as you search for authenticity in work and play.

Now you will turn your sights on the bicycle to see how it reveals the precise actions you will need to take for success.

Chapter 23

Back to the Bicycle

You can find the entire cosmos lurking in its least remarkable objects.

Wislawa Szymborska
Polish poet

Handle Bars = Focus   A concentration so intense it can start a fire.

Seat = Vision   A mental picture, held with faith and gratitude

Front Wheel = Purpose   A fixed intention on doing something important

Back Wheel = Execution   Taking desire fueled purpose & making it happen

Road = Feedback   Joyful Authenticity

Pedals = Desire   Possibility seeking expression

Chain = Commitment   Transforms purpose into reality

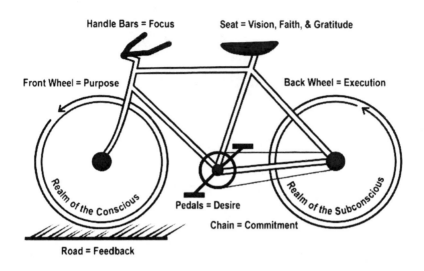

Let me tell you what I think of a bicycle. I think it has done more to emancipate women than anything else in the world. It gives women a feeling of freedom and self-reliance. I stand and rejoice every time I see a woman ride by on a wheel ... the picture of untrammeled womanhood.

Susan B. Anthony
American social reformer and women's rights advocate

The bicycle: Here is how the simple and easily understood bicycle embodies the formula and characterizes the components of success, all while staying in balance with the universe's principles and laws. Once your vision, purpose, and burning desire, are aligned with universal law you are on your way to realizing your authentic self. Moreover, these same principles that are being used here to find your vocation will be the exact principles you will employ to reap success in your chosen endeavor. This process works faithfully, no matter what it is you are striving to achieve.

How?

In your mind's eye, imagine yourself bicycling at this very moment. You mount your bicycle seat with a firmness of vision to find your genuine work. Before finding your stride it's important to be grateful for all the wonderful blessings that have already been bestowed upon you. No matter what your current circumstances are, you have many blessings and they must be acknowledged and appreciated. If you cannot bring yourself to be grateful for what you already have, you might as well stop reading—nothing that follows can really take you another step forward. Fortunately, you have already read a lot to this point, and no doubt some seeds of possibility and growth have been sown.

Once sincere gratitude prevails, your next step will be the development of faith. The person who can sincerely thank God for the things they already own—and for the things which as yet they own only in their imagination—has real faith. There is no substitute for authentic faith, nor can it be provided by anyone but you.

You grasp the handlebars with focus as directed by your *will*. Your purpose—which emanates from your *spirit-inspired will*—is symbolized by the front wheel of your bicycle. The thoughts directed toward your purpose are the creative and constant force that causes a universal power to spring into action. The thing you want is brought to you by your thoughts. By action you receive it. This is why you should be figuratively bicycling at this point—and not simply thinking and mechanically reading—as understandably may be your habit.

The answer to prayer is not according to your faith while you are thinking, but according to your faith while you are doing.

Wallace D. Wattles
American author

A desire presupposes the possibility of action to achieve it.

Ayn Rand
Novelist and philosopher

Desire is represented by the bicycle's pedals, which first establish a toehold and then a foothold toward reaching your true purpose. Desire invigorates your innate powers and fuels the action necessary to actually take you to a place of importance. Where there is no power to do a thing, there will be no desire. Therefore, you need only concern yourself with your natural desire. You have no need to manufacture any worthy desire as you begin to exert force on the pedals of desire. Furthermore, it is important to recognize that your desire can only be exercised by taking action in the present moment. You cannot act where you have been, and you cannot act where you are going to be. You can only act where you are, because this is where your power resides. Once in action, you will begin to bring into existence what it is you are thinking, as dictated by the Law of Attraction.

The back wheel represents the execution of your vision and purpose. This houses the realm of your subconscious mind. You have already learned that the back wheel subconsciously performs in the manner in which it has been programmed by the conscious mind. This happens just as assuredly as corn can only spring from a seed of corn.

To recap, the conscious mind is represented by the seat you occupy, the handlebars you grip, and the purposed front wheel that is headed in its proper direction. At the same time, the pedals of the bicycle joyfully exercise your desire. The chain of commitment—as driven by your vision and desire—is the causal link to the subconscious, which houses powers of immense proportion. The subconscious mind is so named because it acts without our conscious knowledge, like the beating of your heart as you read these words. You have learned that thoughts are causes and our conditions are its effects. Since inauthentic work conditions are produced by our thoughts, they can also be erased by thoughts.

To reiterate, there is no higher science of study than that of proper thinking, so its study and application should be your highest priority. The act of correct thinking spawns all correct action. The laws governing thought are as definite and unwavering as any natural or physical law. This process always works and with the same precision. These metaphysical laws are being represented by the bicycle's frame and dynamics, which makes it more fully comprehensible for all who desire to understand. Understanding comes before use. The real secret of power is being conscious of it, and as you become more aware of this power, you can more easily begin to draw upon it.

There is no doubt that everyone wants to find and follow their best work. This universally shared desire creates our ability to act upon the universal mind and its creative substance. With this in mind, you can be certain that whatever you think will be produced or created in your objective world. The businessman and author Charles Haanel said that we become the equivalent of a live wire as we connect at will to the universal mind.

As you exercise these principles, keep in mind that you can only advance by being larger than your present place. The world is advanced only by those who more than fill their present places. And it is certain that you were designed to advance, as your eyes have been placed in your forehead, and not in the back of your head. Nature, our ever-present model, tells of no fully developed mollusk having to abandon its magnificent and beautiful shell to seek smaller quarters because it has grown smaller. And now as you begin to feel the engine of your destiny, you advance with the light air of anticipation of what lies in front of you, while laying aside troubled memories that have weighed you down. The beautiful butterfly, mentioned earlier, never wishes to carry through life the inhibiting and bothersome cocoon from whence it came.

To Review

Idealize what you are seeking to be, do, or have with a firmness of vision. This harnesses the law of attraction while inspiring an impulse to action. This follows the universal laws of nature. Once fully understood, the laws of nature will remain your vigilant instructor long after you have finished reading this book. Even if finding your authentic work takes time, and it will, there is comfort in knowing that you will never be without your faithful teacher, nature. After all, it constantly displays its immutable laws. Furthermore, you need only to ride a bicycle—or even picture a bicycle in your mind's eye—to be instantly reminded of the formula and components necessary for success at any endeavor, as advocated in this book. Accept that finding your work may indeed take some time. This is not a magic book describing a magic show. This means that your thoughts and actions—as directed by your *will*—have to operate in the real world of education, commerce, and trade, and along their already established lines and channels. This is where universal mind and the cosmic laws butt up against the practical world we all inhabit.

And finally, your day-to-day guiding principle, in whatever professional area of operation you choose, is the *giving of service*. In the end, service is the only legal tender recognized by the universe, and you must open your own personal account. You can be certain that, as you deliver unique and personal service through the vehicle of your authentic work, each and every deposit will be correctly tallied.

Nature teaches you the Law of Attraction, the Law of Creative Power, the Law of Abundance, the Law of Equal and Opposite Reaction, and the Law of Supply and Demand. These and other laws rule the natural world. They are also reflected in the human world of thought. To put these universal laws into practice, the Swedish philosopher Emanuel Swedenborg said, "One must have knowledge of your power, the courage to dare and the faith to do." Power depends on the consciousness of power for unless you use it, you lose it. And unless you are conscious of it, you simply cannot use it. Moreover, your power to think is a spiritual power and this power is creative: it is not competitive, but solely creative.

This should all sound like good news, because it is exactly that. These universal laws that give you the power to reap its fruits are all precise and never vary. For example, if a bridge collapses you do not attribute the fact to a change in the law of gravity. If a light doesn't appear when you flip on an electrical switch, you do not say the laws of electricity cannot be relied upon. Likewise, when every item considered in your mind does not come into being at the moment you think of it, you do not surmise that the Law of Attraction is impotent.

This whole process of finding your best work begins with a firmness of vision and purpose. It is fueled by the power of focus and attention. When your vision is infused with feeling, you are creating the desire necessary to succeed. This desire enhances your concentration, which in turn produces a force of such proportion that it will wrench any secret from nature. Put your heart into the task of finding your work and you will meet with unparalleled success.

Once your work is discovered, the real secret of enduring success will be to give what it is you have. And when you have your heart in your work, you can easily give. Eventually, the more you give, the more you will receive. Again, this is not *Life is a Bicycle* talking, it's nature talking. In Ralph Waldo Emerson's *Essay on Compensation*, he demonstrated how compensation is the way of the universe. Emerson said nature is constantly seeking to strike equilibrium. When something is sent out and provided for, something else must be received. Otherwise a vacuum will be created, and nature abhors a vacuum. And furthermore, your heart naturally desires to give. A heart that does not want to give is abnormal.

Once your authenticity is found, you happily provide the service, product, and what you create, to an awaiting world. Doing so greets you with unparalleled success. In addition—and this is important—as you do the work you love, make sure you harbor the mindset that you wish to create a *use value* that exceeds any *cash value* to be received. This arrangement ensures that every transaction will make for more life to all and less to none, as advocated by Wallace D. Wattles in *The Science of Getting Rich*.

Cycling your metaphysical bicycle aligns your thoughts, desires, and energies with the constitutional essence of the cosmos. The chain of the bicycle represents the continuity of a circuit, and through its rotation is the causal link between the conscious elements of the bicycle's seat, handlebars, front wheel, and pedals, and the *universal mind's* subconscious realm, as represented by the back wheel of the bicycle. At this point the process is completed and the formula is executed. The only things left to do are to be grateful and to appreciate the beauty of the world. You are cycling down a path that pings back images of genuine and legitimate triumph that you have dreamed of—maybe for a long time. You cycle upon a proper path; secured into an authentic orbit that is unique to you. You are at once and forever a bona fide part of the beauty that is your world. The world's beauty ceases to stop at the border of your skin as you graciously work from a place—a core—of authenticity.

This process oils and facilitates the free movement of the once-irregular pistons of Picasso's engine. The bicycle has the unique ability to demonstrate the elements necessary for success. This happens while embodying the universal laws that inextricably guide your efforts to discover your noble work. And once your work is discovered, the exact same bicycling principles will be employed to bring about success in your chosen field.

Live as you will have wished to have lived when you are dying.

Christian Gellert
German poet

Chapter 24

Paint Your Picture

The final exercise of Part III is to imagine and paint a picture of your ideal life. Imagine for a moment that all the philosophical ideals, enlightening questions, and elucidating principles did exactly as they were designed to do—they worked. Therefore, craft an accurate vision of your ideal professional life. Describe this ideal life as it is now. Remember, your goals have been identified and reached. Professionally, things are how you want them to be. Record your visions and thoughts in as much detail as possible. Take your time and have fun with this activity. In your mind's eye, you are experiencing all that you desire professionally, and by natural extension, throughout your life. You now joyfully cycle your bicycle. What a relief this is; every day a thrill.

As I exercise my defining work, and live my ideal life:

I have become _____

I am helping _____

I now enjoy _____

I appreciate _____

I am thankful for _____

I am (whatever you choose) _____ it's *your book now.*

Imagination is the workshop of the soul...Good health, a sense of well being, and a purpose for living make any day beautiful.

Napoleon Hill
American author

An aim in life is the only fortune worth finding.

Robert Louis Stevenson
Scottish writer

Part IV

Finding Your Bicycle

Whenever I see an adult on a bicycle, I have hope for the human race.

H. G. Wells
English writer

A man must love a thing very much if he not only practices it without and hope of fame and money, but even... without any hope of doing it well.

Oliver Herford
American writer & artist

If you follow your Bliss; you put yourself on a kind of track, which has been there all the while waiting for you, and the life that you ought to be living is the one you are living. Wherever you are—if you are following your bliss, you are enjoying that refreshment, that life within you, all the time.

Joseph Campbell
American author

Chapter 25

Elements, Qualities, and Achieving Flow

Introduction

You will never succeed while smarting under the drudgery of your occupation, if you are constantly haunted with the idea that you could succeed better at something else.

Orison Swett Marden
American writer and publisher

Go confidently in the direction of your dreams. Live the life you have imagined.

Henry David Thoreau
American author

A review of where *Life is a Bicycle* has taken you so far in your reading. To accomplish and achieve *authenticity* in life and work, one must live and work from their *nature*. A person who actually lives and works from their *nature* is one who believes in, and senses the pull and power of their *will*. To feel one's *will* one must be in tune with an *essence* that exists in support of this *will*. This *essence* has its genesis in one's *spirit* and the *spirit* is grounded in the *soul*.

199

Your soul's creator exercised their *will* when they created you—created the universe—and its immutable laws, as exhibited in *nature* <u>itself</u>. Your creator infused your *spirit* with an *essence* that can be found in the heart of every living thing. Your *essence* is the foundational building block of your *nature*, leading you to what it is you *will*. You soul's creator is the creator of everything seen in Nature, and likewise is the creator of your *nature*. Your <u>soul</u>'s creator operates from a place of *authenticity* and so should you.

When you experience the beauty of discovering your professional true north, all the angels smile. Just like Sisyphus, you are destined and fated to a life of some type of work. You cannot escape this, nor should you even wish to do so. All of the freedoms and modern conveniences we may take for granted were created by an inspired and enterprising person. All of what you enjoy and possess came from *work* that has preceded you. And it will be ambitious and creative work that moves you forward from here.

John F. Kennedy could have had a life of leisure, considering the magnitude of his family's inheritance. But he did not choose this path. Instead Kennedy vied for and won one of the toughest jobs on the planet. At one time he said something to the effect that a life of leisure is the hardest work there is. And he didn't choose it because he didn't feel he was up to the task.

As you draw closer to finding and following your work, you may sense that you are on the right track. But how can you really know? Are there certain attributes or signs that will give you a degree of comfort, telling you that yes, you are on an authentic professional path? This is a very specific question that can lead to an unambiguous answer. Therefore, let's examine the key elements and attributes found in a true and rewarding professional endeavor. These elements and qualities certify that the work you've chosen is truly yours. Each of these will act as a guidepost, ensuring you have chosen your proper professional path. Knowing you are on your way to riding your bicycle is one of life's most joyous sensations. It is during this time that the mantle of doubt and the malaise of disingenuousness finally fall away.

Habit rules the unreflecting herd.

William Wordsworth
English poet

The test of a vocation is the love of the drudgery it involves.

Logan P. Smith
American-born writer

Elements

In *How to Find the Work You Love*, Laurence Boldt outlines four elements that should be found in authentic work. For each of the elements, he recognizes a creative power along with a focusing question. These dynamics will help assist in determining if the work you do is appropriate for you.

The first *element* is **integrity**, for integrity will be a constant companion, as you perform your work. **Integrity**'s *creative power* is **conscience** and the *focusing question* to ask oneself is, **"What speaks to me?"**

Service is the second *element* ingrained into the essence of your work. The ethical reason for any business is service to others. **Service**'s *creative power* is **compassion,** and the *focusing question* helping you identify whether your bicycle's service's an area of importance to you is, **"What touches me?"**

The third *element* is **enjoyment**. No matter the rigors or pressures of your work there is enjoyment. The *creative power* that naturally fosters enjoyment is **talent,** meaning your talents are exercised and displayed while performing your work. The *focusing question* for enjoyment is, **"What turns me on?"**

> *To enjoy something is to delight in something—to delight in something—one must be paying attention.*

Georgia O'Keefe
American painter

The fourth and final *element* present when bicycling is **excellence. Excellence**'s *creative force* is **destiny** and the *focusing question* is, **"What draws out my best?"**

Review these elements, their creative force, and the accompanying focusing questions as outlined by Laurence Boldt. You have learned that Picasso's engine can only be felt and not seen. Therefore, it is appropriate that these focusing questions can only be answered with one's heart. Your subconscious is already working on answering the vital question: is the work you've chosen—or will choose soon—really the work for you?

*Blessedness.... This is the perfect joy which characterizes
perfect self-activity.*

Baruch Spinoza
Dutch philosopher

Qualities

In *The Outliers,* Malcolm Gladwell described three qualities present in proper work. The first quality is **autonomy**. Autonomy indicates control—at least a measure of control—over your time and effort as you strive to accomplish your purpose. Autonomy implies that you have the opportunity to make your own decisions and utilize discretion. You feel yourself in your work, at least to a degree. You are your own best boss in a very real sense.

Complexity is a second quality present in your work of choice. Complexity means your intelligence and imagination come into play, while exercising your sense of judgment. Your pedaling is not mundane and chockfull of routine tasks. You make decisions and adjustments that correspond to the ever-changing terrain and conditions of your working environment. Your cycling or work may even look tedious and boring to the uninitiated, but not to you.

The third quality present in exacting work is one of **connection.** A direct connection exists between how hard and intelligently you are pedaling and how much you earn. Earnings and income arrive in two distinct forms, and both are necessary for living a fulfilling life. The first is monetary income. The second type of earnings can be thought of as psychic income, which has as its depository one's soul.

I am sure that no man can derive more pleasure from money or fame than I do from seeing a pair of basketball goals in some out of the way place.

James Naismith
American inventor of basketball

If you have two loaves of bread, sell one and buy White Hyacinths to feed your soul.

Asian proverb

There is nothing so degrading as the constant anxiety about one's means of livelihood...Money is a sixth sense without which you cannot make a complete use of the other five.

W. Somerset Maugham
British playwright

These elements are evident when a cyclist wakes up each morning with a heart full of anticipation, wishing to get on with the work of the day. Each one is a frequent, if not constant companion in your work.

*In order that people may be happy in their work, these
three things are needed: They must be fit for it. They
must not do too much of it. And they must have a sense of
success in it.*

John Ruskin
English writer

Achieving Flow

*To establish a place of work, where engineers can feel the
joy of technological innovation, be aware of their mission
to society, and work to their hearts content.*

Masaru Ibuka
describing the first purposes of the incorporation of Sony

The final frontier, signifying you have found your ideal work, is characterized by the sensation of *flow*. This phenomenon was defined by the psychologist, Mihaly Csikszentmihalyi in his book titled *Flow*.

*You've been walking in circles, searching. Don't drink by
the water's edge. Throw yourself in.*

Jeanette Berson
American writer

The elements and qualities of proper work should be felt regularly as you perform your chosen work. The sensation of *flow* may be a bit more infrequent. However, experiencing the euphoric state of *flow* confirms that you are indeed exercising an ideal bicycle.

So what is *flow*? Dr. Csikszentmihalyi says, "Being in flow means you are in a state only described as ecstatic. Intensely working on a clearly defined goal, you are receiving immediate feedback on how you're doing. Immersed in the element of flow creates the sensation you don't exist." The sensation of *flow* has been characterized as feeling *lost in time* and as being completely carried away as in a stream; thus the title of *flow* for this highly gratifying working state.

> *When I am in my painting, I'm not aware of what I'm doing.*

Jackson Pollock
American painter

Obtaining this sensation usually requires that you have a certain level of skill—either learned or natural—in addition to an acquired level of proficiency after years of practice and applying your knowledge. When experiencing *flow*, you don't want to stop your work because everything is going so well. You may not even notice you are hungry as you work for hours, endlessly. In *flow*, you don't think, in a traditional sense, about what you're doing.

Mihaly Csikszentmihalyi describes the seven conditions present when one is in, or experiencing *flow*:

1. Being completely involved in what we are doing, focused, concentrated

2. A sense of ecstasy—of being outside reality

3. Great inner clarity—knowing what needs to be done, and how well we are doing

4. Knowing that the activity is doable—that our skills are adequate to the task, even though the activity may be difficult

5. A sense of serenity—no worries about oneself

6. Timelessness—thoroughly focused on the present, hours seem to pass by in minutes

7. Intrinsic motivation—whatever produces Flow becomes its own reward.

The phenomenon of *flow* is most easily realized by artists (i.e. authors, painters, sculptors, etc.) and in the world of professional sports, cinema, and music. However, *flow* can be achieved by anyone who loves his work and is fast becoming a thoroughbred at what they do. *Flow* is possible for everyone. Albert Einstein said he experienced *flow* when he was struggling with defining his Theory of Relativity. In fact, it's possible that Einstein came up with his Special Theory of Relativity while bicycling. This reputedly led him to say, "I thought of that while riding my bicycle." Experiencing the euphoric state of *flow* is a hallmark of authentic work.

The act of bicycling creates *flow,* and this may be one of the veiled reasons why bicycling enjoys such worldwide appeal. The act of bicycling is an act of *flow.*

Definition of Success: Contributing something to the world and being happy about it. You have to enjoy what you are doing. You won't be very good if you don't and second you have to feel you are contributing something worthwhile. If either of these two ingredients are absent there's probably some lack of meaning in your work.

Norman Augustine
American businessman

Look for your passion, what makes you excited? What turns you on? Find an organization that moves your spirit, if you can.

Anita Roddick
British businesswoman and founder of The Body Shop

Part V

Enjoying Your Bicycle

Cycling through mountains of success and valleys of failure always beats one long desert.

In the matter of two days...I had raised myself master of the most remarkable, ingenious, and inspiring motor ever devised upon the planet.

Frances E. Willard
American activist speaking of learning to bicycle

The man who is dissatisfied with himself, what can he not do?

Henry David Thoreau
American writer

Chapter 26

The Ride of Your Life

*But do your work, and I shall know you: Do your work,
and you shall reinforce yourself.*

Ralph Waldo Emerson
American writer

*To enjoy—to love a thing for its own sake, and for no
other reason.*

Leonardo da Vinci
Italian inventor and artist

The joy found in genuine work shears society's conditioned orbit of conformity. Your true and original nature is reclaimed through the discovery of your defining work. The rosebush—which beautifully works in a season of growth—creates roses because it has absolutely no choice in the matter. The rosebush never over-thinks its role in the world and, in a miscarriage of nature, produces grapes. Yet somehow in our world the unfolding of one's nature ironically becomes more obtuse, although very possible for the dedicated bicyclist.

Once your essence, nature, and talents become aligned with your daily work, a sense of serenity will prevail. No longer do you force yourself through sheer will power to do what you loathe, having transcended the habitual and common working life. Your work runs through your blood and brings to life a great purpose so true and commanding it must be exercised. Authenticity of this magnitude is so rare, but it is the dream of so many.

As you swim among a sea of people seeking inspiration, a supply arrives that corresponds with your demand. You now tap into this supply that was there all along. No longer do you find yourself standing on a shaky and insincere platform, smarting under the dread of spiritless work.

According to James Allen, as you enjoy your cycling adventure, you are "no longer just a thermometer, being transported through life as a straw in a sometimes calm and sometimes raging stream." You cease being a puppet performing on someone else's stage. Your feet are no longer tethered to the pedals of an inauthentic bicycle that is pointlessly void of anything that honestly speaks to you. The exasperating exercise of driving God-given ambition back upon itself comes to an end.

To be nobody but yourself—in a world which is doing it best, night and day to make you everybody else—means to fight the hardest battle which any human can fight, and to never stop fighting.

E. E. Cummings
American poet

You awaken each day as your true self, perhaps for the first time. You proceed with joy and vigor through the days of your life. You know it, and the world knows it.

*If you can fill the unforgiving minute with sixty seconds
worth of distance run, yours is the Earth and everything
that's in it....*

Rudyard Kipling

British writer and poet - Brother Square-Toes—Rewards and Fairies (If)

Authentic work requires energy and effort to the same degree as any
other work you have ever done. Sure you're excited, but your day is not
hurried or rushed as you finally give vent to a grand passion. The longing
for a more satisfying place and time ceases, as your long-slumbering
faculties awaken to your new ambition. You are enjoying—possibly for
the first time—your life.

In *As a Man Thinketh*, James Allen stated:

> *When you were first learning to walk, after numerous attempts
> and falls, you had to enter the way of power by first attempting
> to stand alone. Break away from the tyranny of custom, tradition,
> conventionality, and the opinions of others, until you succeed in
> walking lonely and erect among men. Rely upon your own judgment;
> be true to your own conscience; follow the light that is within you; all
> the outward lights are so many will-o-the-wisps. Therefore, pursue
> your course bravely. Your conscience is at least your own, and to
> follow it is to be a man (and woman); to follow the conscience of
> another is to be a slave.*

You are elated to be one of the rare few who can look the world squarely
in its face and confidently smile. You will never again be self-mocked
by your own ambition. You have come to recognize with a profound
understanding that while you may have found some financial success

in the past, it may not have been the work your spirit sought. Ralph
Waldo Emerson, one of the leading torchbearers in this book, told us that
money often costs too much.

Money can't buy life.

Bob Marley
Reggae musician—last words to son Ziggy

*Money is the string with which a sardonic destiny directs
the motions of the puppets.*

W. Somerset Maugham
British playwright

*Money is human happiness in the abstract. He then, who
is no longer capable of enjoying human happiness in the
concrete devotes himself utterly to money.*

Arthur Schopenhauer
German philosopher

In spite of former financial and professional success, something was
staring into your soul that demanded to be confronted and addressed. It
sought to live a true and sincere life. Fortunately, you successfully failed
to drive the thought of performing your best out of your mind. This
thought became your constant companion that you surely appreciated, but
at times may have resented. You held tight to your never-ceasing search

for authentic work that clearly demonstrates to the world—this is what I think, how I grow, what I dream, and as a result, create. This was the source of a steady *drone* in the recesses of your soul. It was a cadence that built in volume and velocity, ultimately demanding action. Anything less only continued a life of insincerity. You would not be tried, found guilty, and sentenced a lifetime to an excruciating form of self-immolation. Self-respect and integrity compelled you to seek out your best.

> *Two roads diverged in a yellow wood,*
> *And sorry, I could not travel both*
> *And be one traveler....*
> *I shall be telling this with a sigh*
> *Somewhere ages and ages hence:*
> *Two roads diverged in a wood, and I,*
> *I took the one less traveled by,*
> *And that has made all the difference.*

Robert Frost
American poet - The Road Not Taken

The advice of Robert Frost points us down a road that is paved with sincerity. The English poet Lord Byron takes this thought a step further by stating "There is a pleasure in the pathless woods." And Ralph Waldo Emerson instructed you to go "where there is no path and leave a trail."

The invisible engine you read about in the first line of the first chapter of this book radiates a shining purpose. Upon reading that line, you were instantly aware that this engine did indeed exist and you—being in a mindset of discovery—unsurprisingly created room for its discovery. Your unceasing demand created the vigor necessary to feel the latent energy of your spinning engine trying its best to weave the helix of your professional DNA.

The purpose of this book is to help you find unparalleled and authentic work. This does not result from rigid and exacting formulas, but simple illumination of cause and effect. Your *thinking* is the cause and your conditions of employment are the effects.

Hell, there are no rules here. We're trying to accomplish something.

Thomas Edison
American inventor

A universal goal for every worker is wealth, or at least the earning of money. It is interesting how the dominant aim of work can—by a simple twist of fate—be inherited without any work at all. However, the wisdom, confidence, satisfaction, and joy that always accompany truly authentic work can never be obtained by way of an inheritance. Therefore, you must think for yourself and come to your own conclusion, as no man or woman can employ someone else to doing their thinking.

It is only a man's fundamental thoughts that have truth and life in them. For it is these that he really and completely understands. To read the thoughts of others is like taking the remains of someone else's meal, like putting on the discarded cloths of a stranger.

Arthur Schopenhauer

German philosopher

The French author Marcel Proust said, "We don't receive wisdom, we must discover it for ourselves after a journey that no one can take for us or spare us."

You cannot teach a man anything, you can only help him discover it in himself.

Galileo Galilei

Italian scientist

Finding one's authenticity is a great ideal of the highest order. It is so easy to simply read these words. But to come to your conclusion, feel your engine, and ultimately arrive at your own answer, you have to be willing to mount your bicycle and exert pressure on the pedals. At the *end of the day*, you must do your own thinking. You must gain the self-awareness necessary to feel the urges of your engine, including its appetites and desires. You are the only one capable of finding your true self. There is absolutely no one else to listen to. As a child, it never occurred to you to send a friend or sibling to take your first bicycle riding lesson.

Everyone gets the experience; some get the lesson.

T. S. Eliot

British essayist and publisher

Epilogue

Where was I going? I puzzled and wondered about it till I actually enjoyed the puzzlement and wondering.

Carl Sandburg
American poet

I want to be cured of a craving for something I cannot find, and of the shame of never finding it.

T. S. Elliot
British essayist and publisher

Having been a long-time sufferer in a state of professional *inauthenticity* makes me uncommonly qualified to address this subject. Today, as on most days for the last 25 years, I will ride my bicycle—literally. I have pedaled, contemplated, and examined my life while riding my bicycle for well over 25,000 miles. Through mile after mile of personal reflection (thank goodness, I've never had an accident), I marveled at the idea that I am in search of my purposeful and defining engine that I had learned about from Picasso as I rode my bicycle, as both its passenger and engine. Upon finding this arrangement strange and revealing, an impression was etched into my imagination. I found myself inspired and driven to answer the riddle of how one goes about finding their authentic work. The visible labor of my bicycling, along with the invisible labor of my thinking, instilled a euphoric high that I wished to escape to constantly. When I commenced the work of researching and writing *Life is a Bicycle*, I found myself in the same satisfying and sometimes euphoric state of mind.

This intuition—or maybe merely the thought—that the bicycle could be an illuminating metaphor for the act of work first came to me atop my bicycle in October 1991, while cycling around Lake Minnetonka in Minnesota. Finally, in the year 2002 I began to record my thoughts in a journal upon returning from cycling excursions in and around my family's new home in Williamsburg, Virginia. I listened and I wrote, while trying my best to understand the nature of this engine driving me toward something. I have many faults and flaws, but I am not a quitter. My anchoring thought that people are entitled to find and follow their most congenial work was surely congruent with the wishes of the heavens. After all, it's hard to imagine Nature's Creator ever experiencing a bad day of work. My vision for this book came to me with such force and repetitiveness, that I had no place to hide. Thus, I began the painstaking task of writing this book. I quickly grew confident that this was a large idea and I loved it. I soon gathered the knowledge and tools necessary to discover my work, and by extension, my life. It felt good to be finally throwing punches for something I believed in.

Many times during this process I approached a state of exhaustion. This was not physical exhaustion from actually cycling, but mental and emotional fatigue from posing the question, "**Who's riding my bicycle?**" I wondered to myself, "How do I discover work that reflects my nature and values?" As I cycled my bike, I pondered the fact that I was riding a bicycle, but someone, somewhere—was riding *my bicycle*. Who were they? Where did they live? How did they think and what did they enjoy?

I came to realize that I was attracted to people—past and present— who reflected my own nature. I was neutral at best and repelled at worst by the others who didn't. My attraction to people and ideas that illustrated and reinforced my nature was a touchstone that guided my efforts. I became ultra-sensitive to philosophical concepts that resonated with me. Their source didn't matter. I was always raised to be blind to race, nationality, profession, and political interest, or any other category one uses to sort and label people and their ideas as being worthwhile or not. As I dove into my research, I realized I wanted to communicate my findings to any audience available. And the simple reason was that my nature demands it. Finally, I had begun to earnestly listen and make it so. The aim of helping others, discover their fit and congenial work, agrees with my nature. As the philosopher Spinoza explained, "The man who is most useful to me is one who entirely acts from the laws of his own nature."

Those that have suffered understand suffering and therefore, extend their hand.

Patti Smith
American musician

My search for work and authenticity turned into my Sisyphean rock. So here I toiled every day, attempting to find or create a formula to be duplicated by anyone wishing to find blissful, rewarding work. The actual accomplishment of finding and following one's genuine work seemed so rare. It appeared that most of the working world deemed it as oddly out of reach. However, I was willing to investigate this situation under an intense light, and my nature was comfortable with the task. Is this a striking example of my invisible engine at work? Yes, but I could only faintly sense this during the early stages of my writing.

Where there is much light the shadow is deep.

Goethe
German philosopher

Feeling it was my God-given right to discover my true self; I read and investigated what great minds had to say on this topic. I amassed the methods, extrapolated the philosophy, and organized the principles that came to comprise this book. My endless cycling figuratively churned a mixture of thought that I used to establish the backbone and framework of this book. As my creation slowly came into view, I patiently tried to capture the essence of what it wished to express.

Life itself is conceived as a sort of listening.

Walter Pater
English critic

Being a teacher at heart, I wondered if my search and discovery could be organized into a format that would serve two purposes at once: to transform my newfound understanding into personal success, and to create a body of knowledge that would benefit others.

Be a candle or the mirror that reflects it.

Edith Wharton
American novelist

A teacher is like a candle, it consumes itself as it lights the way for others.

Mustafa Kemal Ataturk
First president of Turkey

Appreciating the fact that I could not place people, one by one, into their perfect jobs, and lacking the ability to analyze people to know what work they should undertake, I simply did what I could. My only job was to write a book designed to inspire readers to take intelligent action and claim for themselves their singular work. Once my commitment to this task was absolute, an omnipotent intelligence emerged, supplying me with the resources necessary to complete this mission. I learned firsthand that supply arrives to fill every sincere and legitimate demand. This phenomenon was expressed by Brazilian writer Paulo Coelho when he said, "When you want something, all the universe conspires in helping you to achieve it." My purpose for writing this book was to codify what I was learning. I believed that if the information helped me, it could potentially help you. The simple bicycle—literally under my feet—became the codifier of what I was learning. *Life is a Bicycle* aspires to reduce the time and effort necessary to discover one's ideal work: the cornerstone of an idyllic and meaningful life.

It was Socrates who declared, "The unexamined life is not worth living." However, if examining your life becomes an obsession—as it did for me—you will soon find the over-examined life is not worth living either.

Life has taught me to think, but thinking has not taught me to live.

Alexander Herzen
Russian writer

Before I began to research and write this book, I awoke each day wishing to simply be true to my nature: someone who unfortunately only existed in my mind's eye.

Would it be possible that I should not in any degree succeed? I can scarcely think so. Ah delusive hope, how much further wilt thou lead me?

John James Audubon
French-American painter

I wanted only to live in accord with the promptings which came from my true self. Why was that so very difficult?

Hermann Hesse
German writer

I found myself arduously wading through an undercurrent of frustration that stretched to the horizon, because of a longing and uneasiness in my work. This was not because I was *not* waking up as myself each morning, but because I was. I strove to discover the engine driving me to discover my original self; aptly painted by Picasso as something one never gets to see. Finally, by merging ageless philosophical ideology with practical exercises—all represented symbolically by my bicycle—I discovered my work. Quite literally, the formula as outlined in the pages of this book began to work for me. I realized that Richard Bach was right when he said, "You teach best what you most need to learn."

I realize now that discerning the formula for discovering work that's capable of unfolding your soul is a massive undertaking. This is fine, because we have learned in this book that large ideas have the power to eliminate smaller ones, including the petty obstacles constantly arriving that can shake one's purpose.

A suffering man ought really to consume his own smoke; there is no good in emitting smoke till you have made it into a fire.

Thomas Carlyle
Scottish philosopher

In the end, we ultimately become the photographs we have imprinted upon our subconscious minds, and through intelligent effort your proper image will be developed and materialize. Every act you take from this page forward may be another blow of the chisel that beautifies your image. Discovering your true work is an effect, and by now you have ascertained the cause. To obtain the effect for you and make it real, you must initiate the causes as outlined in this book.

Discover your work and live your unique life in mind, body, and spirit. Determining who is riding your bicycle is worth whatever effort it takes. Writing this book was, without question, the cycling adventure I was seeking. It embraces a personal confirmation of sorts. It clearly confirms that my work here was not done solely for money. Admittedly, this book is well meant, more than well written. However, a psychological independence was my initial goal. I have tasted it and I know. Like any author, I do wish for this book to be published, to sell, and to sell well. I want each book sold to exemplify a business transaction that adds life and happiness to every buyer. If this comes to pass, my work will produce a *use value* that I would deem greater than any *cash value* a reader will ever pay for it, no matter the price a purveyor of this work wishes to charge.

There is only the trying. The rest is not our business.

T.S. Elliot
British essayist and publisher

The essential support and encouragement come from within, arising out of the mad notion that your society needs to know what only you can teach.

John Updike
American novelist

My final encouragement to you is to never stop searching for your authentic work. Above all, enjoy the ride, for at the end of the day that's all we really have. You've spent valuable time reading, journaling, dreaming, and perhaps even fretting over anxious beliefs. All the while, you have likely asked yourself, "Will I ever actually find my genuine work?

If you don't change your beliefs, your life will be like this forever. Is that good news?

W. Somerset Maugham
British playwright

Wherever you go from here, be sure to accomplish what you set out to do when you chose to read this book. Paradoxically, once you choose your work, you will feel your work has actually chosen you.

I don't know if I chose basketball, or if basketball chose me.

Jerry West
NBA legend

I never had to choose a subject—My subject rather chose me.

Ernest Hemingway
American writer

Thy lot or portion of life is seeking after thee; therefore be at rest from seeking after it.

Caliph Ali
Muslim leader

As you blissfully cycle through your life, the years upon reflection may feel more like minutes. When reminded that a particular year was her 25th wedding anniversary, Nancy Reagan commented, as she did on each anniversary, that it had actually felt like 25 minutes. Enjoy every minute you're allowed to perform the beautiful work for which you were created. Plato defined something as beautiful if it did what it was supposed to do, or if it hit its target. I hope you have found something of beauty in the pages of this book. Each page contains my simple, sincere desire that you will discover the work that you were blessed to perform. Then and really only then will you be beautiful to all, because you have become beautiful to yourself.

The bottom line—and if you will indulge one last bicycling analogy—is that your life is a movie that is aptly titled *Breaking Away*. Only in this movie you play the roles of writer, director, and star[2].

As writer, director, and star, your role is analogous to being your bicycle's passenger and engine. The point is that as lead actor and director, you can purposefully *author* the remaining scenes of the movie that is your life. Take a minute and ask yourself how has my movie been playing itself out so far? Is it a thriller, a slow-moving melodrama, a comedy, or a tragedy? Is the narrative structure of this movie—which will get only *one take*—filled with insincere and rambling scenes? Is it poorly scripted and amateurishly spliced together, forever lacking a legitimate theme and purpose? You will know since not only are you the writer, director, and star but always the silent, unflinching critic.

---

2   ***Breaking Away*** is a 1979 movie written by Steve Tesich and directed by Peter Yates. It is number eight on the list of America's 100 Most Inspiring Movies.

If your life had lyrics, would they be any good?

Douglas Coupland
Canadian writer

In his play *As You Like It*, Shakespeare described how, "All the world's a stage, and all the men and women merely players; they have their exits and their entrances; and one man in his time, plays many parts." Though you may be anxious about having only *one take* at your life's movie, keep in mind that over time it will fortunately have many scenes and episodes, and perhaps even an intermission. As the director it is you who holds the power to make the coming acts of your life different from the previous scenes that have already played out. So take control of your life and write your life's play. Become the hero and gracefully watch the world and its myriad of characters take on their roles.

Remember, you are just an extra in everyone else's play.

Franklin D. Roosevelt
U.S. president

Not having discovered your work by your own devices—use the philosophical principles described herein to redirect your life. Transport your positive habits and wonderful traits into the dimension of your new movie set. Enter a purposeful and exciting stage of life that is destined to be a classic that the world can't wait to see. As Bob Dylan's brilliance told me while sitting alone in the dark listening to his music, "Strike another match; go start anew." It's never too late to begin.

I feel that I am entitled to my share of lightheartedness and there is nothing wrong with enjoying one's self simply, like a boy.

Leo Tolstoy

Russian writer - In response to criticism for learning to ride a bicycle at age 67

"Count Leo Tolstoi, the Russian novelist, now rides the Wheel much to the astonishment of the peasants on his estate. A cycling notes entry in *Scientific American* for April 18, 1896"

Life is not a dress rehearsal.

Rose Tremain
English novelist

If life had a second edition, how would I correct the proofs?

John Clare
English poet

As the hero bicycling through your magnificent play, be sure to take nothing for granted. Do not take your health, sense of wonderment, and what attracts your attention for granted. Be grateful for all your blessings—be they known or unknown; seen or unseen; appreciated or unappreciated. Don't take it all in vain. Go to your work and joyfully toil, loving what you do. Make this your reality and resolve to do whatever has to be done for its achievement. Reset and redirect your life using the acumen of an extremely aware, thoughtful, and accomplished bicyclist. Finally, above all else, search until your best is found, and never ever stop pedaling. It is with great anticipation for you and me that I write the last few words of this book.

My final encouragement is to never forget that **life is a bicycle—if you stop pedaling, you'll fall off.** This book ends where it began, with Thomas Carlyle's quote:

Blessed is he who has found his work. Let him ask no other blessing.

When spirits are low, when the days appear dark, when work becomes monotonous, when hope hardly seems worth having, just mount a bicycle and go out for a spin down the road. Without thoughts on anything but the ride you are taking.

Sir Arthur Conan Doyle
Scottish physician and writer

When man invented the bicycle, he reached the peak of his attainments. Here was a machine of precision and balance for the convenience of man and women. And the more he used it, the fitter his body became. Here, for once, was a product of man's brain that was entirely beneficial to those who used it, and no harm or irritation to others. Progress should have stopped when man invented the bicycle.

Elizabeth Howard West
author

I held out my hands over a chasm filled with the fear of never finding my authenticity. In one hand was the question, "What is my purpose, and therefore my work?" In the other hand the question, "How do I find it?" As I placed my hands together the chasm closed and the answer came— from the only place it could—from within my very self.

Garry Fitchett
American writer

This is a day, the lord hath made; Let us rejoice and be glad in it.

Psalm 118:24

A Bible verse often quoted by my Mother

*You're off! Authentically bicycling! And just like your
new and admiring friend Sisyphus, a moon full of dreams
that you are fated to achieve is joyfully fixed atop your
shoulders. Your True North is aligned with your destiny,
directly ahead and clearly in view. Take care.*

Acknowledgements

Thank you to the authors, artists and philosophers providing insight into the art and science of discovering one's authentic work. Your imagination, intellect, and defining perspective provided the tesserae of an illuminating mosaic, answering a mystery that plagues every generation. The inspiration and instruction that filled the pages of this book came from: Albert Camus, Joseph Campbell, Guy Finley, Vernon Howard, Orison Swett Marden, Michael Ventura, Thomas Carlyle, Frances Willard, Mihaly Czikzentmihalyi, Ralph Waldo Emerson, Henry David Thoreau, Malcolm Gladwell, Baruch Spinoza, Charles Haanel, Laurence Boldt, Ayn Rand, Pablo Picasso, Leonardo da Vinci, James Allen, Abraham Maslow, Arthur Schopenhauer, and many others, each shedding their ray of light on this enthralling topic.

Thank you to my wife, Julie, for reviewing, editing, and having to suffer through my first feeble attempts to put into print a consuming fire that raged in my heart and mind. I remember my frustration as you examined those initial drafts and could never find three consecutive words that did not demand revision. Thank you to Bob and Shirley Saunders for taking the time to review early drafts of the book. Bob is a retired history professor at Christopher Newport University and an author. He and Shirley offered many suggestions for improvement, along with providing much-needed encouragement that this project was worthwhile. In addition, I want to thank Tom Hardin, the Editor of the Southside Sentinel, which is the weekly newspaper in my hometown of Urbanna, Virginia. Tom reviewed a near-completed version of this work and offered valuable feedback. Furthermore, and with tremendous gratitude, I praise the detailed work of my editor Chris Guthrie of Open Book Editors for his invaluable contribution. A special thanks to my neighbor Walter for referring to me as Larry Darrell. And thank you Kipper for being by my side for every word.

Finally, I thank the scores of book publishers who said *no* to this book proposal—a few repeatedly—and who took the time to inform me by way of a rejection letter. Many of your letters started with the salutation— *Dear Author*. I remember smiling as I opened that first one. No one had ever referred to me as an author until that first moment of rejection. Ironically, receiving those letters only inspired me further toward my vision. But most importantly, I thank Morgan James Publishing, David Hancock, Cindy and David Sauer and their team, for saying *yes*.

About the Author

Garry F. Fitchett lives with his wife, Julie, and his sons, Dylan and John, in Williamsburg, Virginia. After receiving a master's degree in education from the University of North Carolina at Chapel Hill, he chose to follow his heart and became a business executive. He followed this by co-owning a business development company with his brother, John. Although successful, he longed to find true and deeply meaningful work that he felt would display his authenticity.

In the spring of 2012, after selling his business, he embarked on a three-year intellectual sojourn that crystallized twenty years of research and ultimately defined the process of discovering the ideal work to engage his talents and energy. This book is the culmination of that learning, research, and self-reflection.

Life is a Bicycle—If You Stop Pedaling You'll Fall Off leads the reader through an evolution of thought directing them to their professional best. It blends an entertaining mix of philosophy with practical principles that are designed to enlighten anyone wishing to discover their purpose-filled, value-centered life.

Many of these concepts were formulated as he bicycled over 25,000 miles, contemplating what he felt would be the ultimate task of finding and following his proper work. Enjoy! Garry is the President of Cypress Education, LLC and conducts people management seminars throughout the United States.